INTEGRATION AS INTEGRITY

INTEGRATION AS INTEGRITY

The Christian Therapist as Peacemaker

Cameron Lee, PhD

CONTRIBUTORS:
Terry D. Hargrave, PhD
Pamela Ebstyne King, PhD
Miyoung Yoon Hammer, PhD

CASCADE *Books* · Eugene, Oregon

INTEGRATION AS INTEGRITY
The Christian Therapist as Peacemaker

Fuller School of Psychology Integration Series

Cascade Books
An Imprint of Wipf and Stock Publishers
199 W. 8th Ave., Suite 3
Eugene, OR 97401

www.wipfandstock.com

PAPERBACK ISBN: 978-1-5326-8668-9
HARDCOVER ISBN: 978-1-5326-8669-6
EBOOK ISBN: 978-1-5326-8670-2

Cataloguing-in-Publication data:

Names: Lee, Cameron, author. | Hargrave, Terry, contributor. | King Pamela Ebstyne, contributor. | Hammer, Miyoung Yoon, contributor

Title: Integration as integrity : the Christian therapist as peacemaker / by Cameron Lee; with contributions by Terry D. Hargrave, Pamela Ebstyne King, and Miyoung Yoon Hammer.

Description: Eugene, OR: Cascade Books, 2020 | Series: Fuller School of Psychology Integration Series | Includes bibliographical references and index.

Identifiers: ISBN 978-1-5326-8668-9 (paperback) | ISBN 978-1-5326-8669-6 (hardcover) | ISBN 978-1-5326-8670-2 (ebook)

Subjects: Psychotherapy—Religious aspects—Christianity | Counseling—Religious aspects—Christianity

Classification: BR115.C69 L44 2020 (print) | BR115.C69 (ebook)

Manufactured in the U.S.A.   JANUARY 27, 2020

Dedication

This book is dedicated to all the students of the Marriage and Family program—past, present, and future—at Fuller Seminary. It is a privilege to explore our vocation together.

CONTENTS

SERIES FOREWORD

Fuller School of Psychology
Integration Series

Series editor, Brad D. Strawn, PhD
Evelyn and Frank Freed Professor for
the Integration of Psychology and Theology

The School of Psychology at Fuller Theological Seminary began its unique ministry of training clinical psychologists (PhD) in Pasadena, California, in 1964. The uniqueness of this training was that it was conducted in a seminary where students received an education emphasizing the integration of psychological theory and science with Christian theology. In 1972 the School of Psychology was the first clinical program in a seminary to be accredited by the American Psychological Association. In 1987 the Marriage and Family Ministries program in the School of Theology moved over to the School of Psychology and became the Marriage and Family Therapy program (MFT). In 1988 the school expanded again to include the Doctor of Psychology degree, PsyD.

In those early days (and in certain quarters even today) some wondered what the two disciplines of psychology and theology could say to each other. Some thought it contamination to integrate the two, conceiving psychology as a secular and anti-Christian science. But the pioneers at Fuller School of Psychology disagreed. Rather than taking an adversarial approach, the faculty developed a variety of models for integrative dialogue, conducted empirical research in the psychology of religion, and reflected on working clinically with people of faith. Through it all, Fuller has endeavored to bring the best of Christian theology (faith and practice) into honest conversation with the best of psychology (science and practice).

One of the hallmarks of the Fuller integration project is the annual Fuller Symposium on the Integration of Psychology and Theology, better known as the Integration Symposium. Each year a noted scholar working at the interface of psychology and religion is invited on campus to give a series of three lectures. These lectures include three respondents, one from the School of Psychology, one from the School of Theology, and one from the School of Intercultural Studies. In this way, the lectures and the dialogue that follows continues in this integrative dialogical tradition.

Included in the Fuller School of Psychology Integration Series are works that have emerged from these Integration Symposium Lectures, dissertation projects that have passed with distinction, and integrative projects written by scholars both within and outside the Fuller community. The series endeavors to both preserve the rich tradition of the Integration Symposium as well as create opportunities for new dialogue in the integration of psychology and theology. This volume emerges from the lectures given by Cameron Lee, a member of the Marriage and Family Therapy faculty at Fuller, in 2018.

Other volumes in the series:

Paris, Jenell. *The Good News about Conflict: Transforming Religious Struggle over Sexuality.*

Hoffman, Marie T. *When the Roll is Called: Trauma and the Soul of American Evangelicalism.*

CHAPTER 1

VOCATION, VISION, AND STORY: LIVING INTO SHALOM

Occasionally, I enjoy a good jigsaw puzzle. By temperament, I'm not the most organized person in the world, and tend to take things as they come. But somehow, when it comes to jigsaws, I suddenly become Mr. Methodical. I comb through the box and find all the corner and edge pieces, then study the picture on the box lid and construct the frame. I roughly sort the pieces by color and markings: these have some cloud and sky, while these have grass or trees. As the puzzle progresses, I've even gone as far as to organize the pieces by shape, to make it easier to find the one I need.

There's something strangely gratifying about doing puzzles, about finding pieces that fit together. Slowly but surely, what began as a confused jumble of parts begins to form into an aesthetically pleasing whole. The last piece is triumphantly snapped into place with a flourish, and these days the moment will probably be captured digitally for Facebook or Instagram.

In some ways, the activity that is loosely known as "integration"—the attempt to bring together psychology with Christian faith and theology—is somewhat like that. Much of the work done has been akin to putting together interdisciplinary jigsaw puzzles. We gather pieces that seem like they should fit, work diligently to connect them, and experience a certain aesthetic pleasure in the process. We might even harbor the distant hope that if enough people work together even the biggest puzzle might someday be finished.

Realistically, though, there is a practical limitation to an interdisciplinary approach in which we speak grandly but vaguely of the "integration of psychology and theology," or "psychology and Christianity," or even "psychology and the Christian faith." Using a distinction coined years ago by Steve Bouma-Prediger, the ultimate fruit of an *inter*-disciplinary approach is limited by the lack of *intra*-disciplinary integration on each side; bringing X and Y together into a coherent whole is much more difficult when neither is monolithic nor simple.[1]

On one side, for example, the word "psychology" represents a complex and ever-expanding array of empirical, theoretical, and clinical projects. Ideally, we'd want our therapeutic interventions to be empirically defensible and to proceed clearly from accepted theories. In turn, we'd want our research to help us test and build theory and be clinically relevant. But the truth is that such ideals are not achieved as often or as thoroughly as we might like. Research on clinical outcomes lags far behind the pace of clinical innovation; empirical results accumulate in ways that fail to make clear contributions to the development of theory or therapeutic practice, and so on. Similarly, a word like "theology"—or even more broadly, "faith"—represents not only different branches and emphases in theological study, but a whole gamut of traditions, beliefs, and practices, each with its own distinctive historical roots.

Intra-disciplinary integration, within either psychology or theology, is thus both an ongoing task and an elusive goal because each field is characterized by a kaleidoscopic diversity of interests

---

1. Bouma-Prediger, "Task of Integration."

and perspectives.[2] By extension, *inter*-disciplinary integration is not a single, enormous jigsaw puzzle; it's a thousand puzzles whose interrelationship is often unclear and possibly even unspecifiable. And nobody has a picture on a box to tell us for certain which pieces should go where. That's not to say, of course, that we should abandon our puzzles and cease our interdisciplinary strivings. Creative conversation across our taken-for-granted disciplinary boundaries can be both stimulating and enriching.

But perhaps there are other ways to think about our task. For example, I've been in many meetings in which some change to an institutional policy was proposed and debated—without there first being some clear consensus about why the change was needed, or what problem the proposal was trying to solve. Similarly, we might ask ourselves: if in some ways psychology and theology seem to exist and even thrive in blessed ignorance of each other, why bring them together? Is it just because we enjoy doing puzzles, or is there something more?

What problem, in other words, does this thing called "integration" attempt to solve? Such a question, of course, doesn't have one definitive answer. But what I'd like to propose in these chapters is an answer that expresses the way I've taught integration for many years. In this view, integration is a personal matter of maintaining the *integrity* of one's vocational identity.

That word "integrity" is in need of some explanation. Usually, when we say that a person has integrity, we mean that the person is trustworthy because they do what they say and stick to their moral principles. That's similar to the way integrity, as an ethical ideal, is described by the American Psychological Association: clinicians should aspire to be people who are honest and truthful, who avoid fraud or deception, and who keep their promises.[3]

---

2. I am borrowing the term from Joel Green's essay on the atonement, in which he argues for an irreducible diversity of New Testament motifs for understanding what was accomplished on the cross. Green, "Kaleidoscopic View," 157–85.

3. See Principle C under "General Principles" at http://www.apa.org/ethics/code/.

This is more than just a matter of rule-keeping or maintaining appearances. Integrity requires an underlying unity and consistency of value, belief, and behavior. As one prominent textbook on biomedical ethics defines it, the virtue of integrity entails "a coherent integration of aspects of the self—emotions, aspirations, knowledge, and the like—so that each complements and does not frustrate the others."[4] In a similar vein, I think of integrity as dependent on a kind of *narrative coherence*,[5] and my suggestion here is that graduate education in a seminary environment often leaves students with less coherence than when they began. Let me begin with an experiential description of what I mean.

Every year, I ask my students about the conversations they had with their families and home churches about coming to seminary to study psychology. Were those conversations positive or negative? Encouraging or discouraging? There are always, of course, the naysayers: *If you're going to go to seminary, then fine— study to be a pastor or a missionary. But a therapist? Is that really a Christian thing to do?* There are also those who, while not rejecting the idea, are suspicious of it: *Can you learn to do real therapy in a school like that, or are they just going to teach you to bash people with Bible?* Or the parental version of the question: *If your degree is from a religious school instead of a well-respected secular university, will you be able to get a real job?* The good news, however, is that I've observed a positive trend over time: increasingly, students report that the conversations were by and large supportive. Indeed, many students were encouraged to apply by our alumni. (The only slightly disturbing part of that trend is that more students are also coming to me at the beginning of each year and saying, "Do you remember having so-and-so as a student? That's my mom. She says 'Hi.'")

But even when one begins graduate study riding a wave of optimism, spurred on by the encouragement of family, there's something potentially destabilizing about training to be a therapist, and doing so in the context of a theological seminary. It's

4. Beauchamp and Childress, *Principles of Biomedical Ethics*, 40.

5. Lee, "Integration and the Christian Imagination," 246–64.

not just the experience of having somebody "rock your boat." It's the more fundamental discovery that you have a boat in the first place—more than one, actually—that can be not only rocked, but capsized.

Welcome to seminary, the place where many come to discover their vocation.

ROCKING THE BOAT

I want us to think together for a few moments about boat-rocking, starting with our many and various theological boats. Under the broad umbrella of evangelicalism, our seminary prides itself on its theological diversity. That diversity, however, brings its own personal challenges. Imagine yourself as a student who has never taken a Bible or theology class before. If you're like I was at that stage, raised neither in the church nor a Christian family, you might be ready for anything. Your challenge is not only to understand what you're being taught, but to find a way to make sense of the different things you're being told by different professors.

But let's make the picture a little more complicated. Maybe you were raised as a dyed-in-the-wool five-point Calvinist, and you've just made friends with an Arminian who's disturbed by how you read Paul—and vice versa. Both of you are just now learning the vocabulary to describe the differences between you, even as you discover that categorical distinctions like Calvinist versus Arminian don't quite tell the story. Or you hail from a relatively staid liturgical tradition and keep finding yourself sitting in chapel next to people who insist on raising their hands during worship. And even if you and a classmate come from the same tradition, you may fret over differences in how strongly and personally the two of you are committed to what you were taught. One of you is thinking, "Traitor!" The other is thinking, "Stick in the mud!"

Or you're sitting in a Bible class, and for the first time in your life, you're exposed to the idea that your very favorite psalm—the one you routinely turn to in times of distress!—probably wasn't written by King David. Some of the other students take the news calmly and with a somewhat lofty and doctrinaire attitude, as if to say, "Well, everybody knows *that*." But you're wondering if this means you can't trust your Bible anymore. You're reluctant to say so, because you don't want to sound foolish or out of place. So you cope with the tension the way you did in college: you keep your head down, keep your doubts to yourself, say what you think the professor and the other students want to hear, and settle up with God later.

Pedagogically, professors work hard to broaden students' intellectual horizons and free them from the supposed shackles of parochialism. Some such understanding of the educational task has a long history. But it's easy to forget how even a simple and seemingly harmless bit of broadening can provoke a crisis of meaning, small or large. I remember, for example, explaining the basic meaning of the doctrine of penal substitutionary atonement to someone who replied, "Well, that's what I've always been taught, and that's what I believe. I just didn't know it had a name." Satisfied with my answer, she was about to walk away. Suddenly, however, she realized the implication of there being a theological "it" to name. She turned back to me, and her next question was more anxious: "You mean some Christians *don't* believe that?"

Our theological boats, of course, aren't the only ones to be rocked in graduate school. Exposure to new *psychological* ideas can be personally challenging in its own right, and this too occurs in the context of learning competing schools of thought. I teach a survey course in family systems theory, for example, that covers a potentially dizzying range of approaches, each with its own specialized vocabulary. I know this can be overwhelming, so I try to bring some order to the subject by noting historical links between the ideas and attempting to hold the various approaches together at a meta-theoretical level.

Still, each lecture is also designed to be provocative in its own way. New terminology, after all, makes it possible to name personal behaviors and relationship patterns that had previously gone unnoticed, so I ask questions that prod students to apply the theories to their own lives. On the one hand, the experience can be empowering. On the other, however, the questions can poke painfully at old and incompletely healed wounds, opening a Pandora's Box of anxious thoughts. Similar experiences await in other classes, for self-examination is a necessary albeit uncomfortable part of a clinician's professional development.

Moreover, the potentially destabilizing effect of education can happen even if the professor doesn't encourage personal application of the material. To be a therapist, for example, one must study the DSM—the Diagnostic and Statistical Manual of Mental Disorders—to learn appropriate diagnostic skills.[6] It's one thing to just study and memorize the material, get your grade and move on. It's another to be struck by the depth and variety of ways in which people suffer psychologically, or by the clinical detachment with which such suffering is described. And it's still another to read the DSM and see your own psychological suffering or that of your family members and friends described in its pages.

Education, then, forms us in both positive and negative ways; it constructs and deconstructs, builds up and tears down. Describing this process from another angle, I have sometimes used the following diagram to capture what I believe to be part of the experience of graduate theological education and how it relates to one's background and formation (see Figure 1). The word "theology" in the center of the diagram refers to theology in its more general sense, not limited to the doctrine of God nor to the professional activity of scholars, pastors, or even seminarians. I have in mind something like the opening lines of Stan Grenz's *Theology for the Community of God*, in which theology is or should be understood as an activity of the entire church: "Every Christian is a theologian. Whether consciously or unconsciously, each person of faith embraces a belief system. And each believer, whether in a deliberate manner or merely implicitly, reflects on the content of these beliefs and their significance for the Christian life."[7]

---

6. American Psychiatric Association, *Diagnostic and Statistical Manual of Mental Disorders*.

7. Grenz, *Theology for the Community of God*, 1.

FIGURE 1

The horizontal axis of the diagram represents the fact that this reflection is sometimes done individually, in the privacy of one's own thoughts, and sometimes corporately, as part of our life together as believers. Corporate theological reflection happens not only in the seminary classroom but the Sunday School classroom, in shared liturgy and worship, even in God-focused conversation between friends.

The vertical axis represents the distinction in Grenz's description between what is conscious and what is unconscious, between reflection that is explicit and that which is more implicit. I realize that he was not intending to use the words "conscious" or "unconscious" in any technical psychological sense. But I find the idea of unconscious or implicit "reflection" to be somewhat opaque; the word itself seems biased toward deliberate thought. For that reason, I prefer philosopher Michael Polanyi's distinction between *focal* and *subsidiary* forms of *awareness*.[8]

One of Polanyi's illustrations of the two types of awareness is the activity of driving a nail with a hammer.[9] At a subsidiary level, you're aware of how the hammer feels in your hand—its heft and balance, or even the subtle sensations that tell you that the head may be loose—and you automatically adjust your grip accordingly. Your attention, however, must be focused on the head of the nail. Both forms of awareness work together to help you hit the nail instead of your finger.

A neurologist hearing Polanyi's example might explain it in terms of *proprioception*, the ongoing subconscious awareness of

8. Polanyi, *Personal Knowledge*; Polanyi and Prosch, *Meaning*.

9. Polanyi, *Personal Knowledge*, 55; Polanyi and Prosch, *Meaning*, 33.

where the parts of our bodies are and how they are moving through space. Proprioceptive awareness is subsidiary in the way Polanyi describes; without it, even the most basic tasks would become awkward and laborious. Oliver Sacks, for example, has written poignantly of a young woman named Christina who was struck by a rare and devastating kind of neuropathy. Without proprioception, without any tacit sense of her body, she could no longer walk without focusing visually on her legs, willing first one and then the other to move one small step at a time. If she lost concentration or closed her eyes, she would fall. Even sitting upright in a chair had to be a performance of will instead of an automatic behavior.[10] Polanyi's claim is that all knowing has this tacit dimension. That insight, I believe, helps us understand that the work of integration takes place against the tacit background of our education and formation.

Let's go back to the diagram. Again, with respect to the horizontal axis, there is a dialectical relationship between individual theological reflection and corporate theological conversation. It's easy to imagine how we can be formed by activities with an intentional theological focus. But to this we must add a tacit dimension. One hopes, after all, that explicit theological instruction, whether from the pulpit or the lectern, does more than add to a person's intellectual storehouse of ideas. When we are at our best in our preaching and teaching, we seek to form people's character, to shape their moral and theological imagination at a more subsidiary level. Learning the meaning of penal substitutionary atonement, for example, is not merely for the purpose of passing a theology exam, but for forming lives of deep and abiding wonder at the mercy of God.

There is more than this, however, to our tacit formation. Our theological imagination is shaped by our participation in Christian community even when there is no explicit focus on theology. We may have heard an endless number of sermons about Christian love; perhaps we've even meditated on and memorized 1

10. In the case study, she is referred to as "the disembodied lady." Sacks, *Man Who Mistook His Wife*, 43–54.

Corinthians 13. But what we truly know about love, way down in our spiritual and psychological bones, is also a matter of what we have observed and experienced in community with others. Many students come to seminary having been loved well in their home churches. They had models of faithfulness to admire and emulate. But others spent time in congregations where it was unsafe to speak openly about the lack of congruence between the talk and the walk, between what people professed and how they lived—and this experience was as formative, if not more so, than anything they heard from the pulpit.

One could make similar observations about our *psychological* imagination. How we understand human motivation and behavior is shaped not only by what we read and study, but by the history of our relationships and the folk wisdom of our families and communities. Such folk wisdom can be quite resistant to change, regardless of how much it conflicts with what the textbooks or empirical evidence might say.[11] Moreover, our shared but uncritical use of language makes a difference. Tragically, here in the United States, we have been subjected to an epidemic of school shootings. How do we talk about such things with friends, or in church, or on social media? Do we ever talk about the "nutcase" who went "mental" and shot innocent people? When we do, we reinforce negative stereotypes of the mentally ill as dangerous and unpredictable. Even within our churches, we may have internalized what Marcia Webb has recently called "negative lay theologies of psychological disorder" which too often stigmatize believers who struggle psychologically.[12] I'll say more about the stigma of mental illness in the third chapter. For now, I simply want to note that the conversations I mentioned earlier about what it means to come to seminary to study psychology may occur against the background of such lay theologies of psychological disorder, which may be mostly subsidiary.

Our students, then, come to us having already been formed by their individual and communal experiences. What they hear

11. See Bruner's discussion of "folk psychology" in *Acts of Meaning*, 1–65.

12. Webb, *Toward a Theology of Psychological Disorder*.

in the classroom and read in their books may agree with, extend, complicate, or contradict what they already know, and much of that knowledge may be tacit. Focal conversations and provocative readings and lectures bring what is subsidiary out of the shadows. New ideas give students a language for thoughts that previously had only tiptoed at the edges of awareness, and naming them gives them substance. And again, this is just as true of their psychological training as it is of the theological.

So what does any of this have to do with integration? For Polanyi, the word "integration" points to the relationship between the subsidiary and focal dimensions of knowing. Think, for example, of a concert pianist. Her focus is on the music; she is only tacitly aware of her hands and fingers. But both forms of awareness must be integrated into the performance. If she begins to focus on her fingers instead, even for a moment, the necessary tacit integration will be broken and the performance will falter.[13]

Metaphorically, this describes the situation for many of our students. Figuring out how to reconcile what they consciously learn in psychology and theology can be complicated enough. But it is doubly so when the tacit integration one had previously taken for granted has been undermined by the process of graduate study itself, which forces us to turn our attention from the music to our fingers. And to strain the metaphor just a little further: despite the frequently deconstructive and dis-integrative nature of their educational experience, our students, upon graduation, will interview at and serve in contexts where they may be expected to play like virtuosos.

We can state this in still another way. I'm reminded of what Walter Brueggemann, in his discussion of evangelism, once called the "coherent construal of reality through faith."[14] Through proclamation and imaginative response, people are invited to live into the dramatic narrative of Scripture. Evangelism is not, Brueggemann insists, only for the benefit of those who would be considered "outsiders" to the faith. It is also for the insiders who have

13. Polanyi and Prosch, *Meaning*, 40.

14. Brueggemann, *Biblical Perspectives on Evangelism*, 98.

become passive or disillusioned and need to have their imaginations revitalized. And it is especially for our children, who must be taught "to perceive, embrace, and enact the world according to the peculiar memory and vision of faith held by the gospel community."[15] Thus, in the terms we have been using, one might say that "evangelism," at one level, refers to making the good news an object of focal attention. But the proclamation and practices appropriate to that news must also reach into our imaginations at a subsidiary level, so that we perceive the world in terms of that tacit background and act accordingly—not just individually, but corporately.

I submit, then, that one of the problems that integration must address is the fragmentation of consciousness, imagination, or identity that can accompany the academic experience. This is what I mean by integration as a personal matter of "integrity," understood as a sense of wholeness that is characterized by narrative coherence or coherent construal. Students may come to seminary with a reasonably coherent theological and psychological construal of the world (even if the construal itself is one that professional theologians or psychologists would question in some way). Or perhaps they had such a construal until they stepped outside the orbit of their families and churches and went away to college. To a further extreme, they may never have experienced coherence in the first place. Whichever might be the case for any particular student, I think it fair to say that the graduate school environment itself often leans more toward incoherence than coherence, and that the need for integration is created, in part, by that experience.

I am not, of course, claiming that this is the only way to think about integration. But from a pedagogical standpoint, I believe we must acknowledge the potentially dis-integrative effects of graduate education if we want to form students who have a robust sense of vocation. What remains for this chapter, then, is to explain what I mean by "narrative coherence," what it has to do with vocation, and how both are linked with our overall theme of peacemaking.

15. Brueggemann, *Biblical Perspectives on Evangelism*, 98.

STORY AND VOCATION

First, then, what do I mean by narrative coherence? Anyone who has studied human development, and particularly adolescent development, is acquainted with Erik Erikson's idea that adolescence is a pivotal stage during which identity begins to form.[16] This is an intrinsically meaning-making process which entails, as Dan McAdams has argued, a kind of tentative "historiography" that integrates past and present into a relatively coherent story.[17] Indeed, there is empirical evidence that life narratives typically become increasingly coherent as individuals proceed through adolescence.[18]

But what makes a narrative coherent? Within the literature on life narratives, Tilmann Habermas and Susan Bluck have suggested four different and overlapping types of *global coherence* that may characterize how people understand and tell the story of their lives.[19] Their notion of *biographical coherence*, for example, raises the question of whether an individual's life story coheres with the storytelling norms of his or her cultural context. *Temporal coherence* refers to how the events of a story are ordered in time. *Causal coherence* refers to how well a story makes explanatory links between events and their internal and external causes.[20] Finally, *thematic coherence* refers to how the elements of a life story are joined together by thematic similarities.

It is this final, thematic type of coherence that I want to dwell on for the rest of this chapter. McAdams argues that while the formation of identity narratives properly begins in the teenage years, it doesn't end there; we continue to rewrite our life stories all throughout adulthood.[21] Moreover, these stories are not suddenly created *ex nihilo* when we reach adolescence. Different story

16. Erikson, *Identity, Youth, and Crisis.*

17. McAdams, *Stories We Live By,* 102.

18. Habermas and de Silveira, "Development of Global Coherence."

19. Habermas and Bluck, "Getting a Life."

20. Similarly, see Gergen's notion of "causal linkages" in *Realities and Relationships,* 192.

21. McAdams, *Stories We Live By,* 91.

elements and characteristics are contributed by past experiences. The quality of our attachment relationships in early childhood, for example, influences whether the life stories we form later have a positive or negative tone.[22] In late childhood and on into the adolescent years, we become more concerned with understanding motivations and intentions, with why people do what they do. The story takes on one or more themes, which McAdams describes as "a cluster of narrative content having to do with what characters in the story recurrently want or intend."[23] Such themes help organize an ideologically coherent story that tentatively answers questions about past, present, and future—who have we been, who are we now, and who do we wish to be?

Thus, thinking pedagogically and pastorally about the challenges of seminary education and clinical training, I am proposing an understanding of integration as integrity by raising questions of narrative coherence. And in particular, I am emphasizing the formation of a thematically coherent sense of vocation. Again, let me begin on a more experiential note.

Over the years, I've had many conversations with students about matters of vocation. Some students arrive at seminary with a clear and definite sense of call: *this is what God wants me to do with my life, and this is the place I'm going to learn how to do it, period.* Others, however, are less sure. Previous conversations and experiences have pointed them in this general direction. But they're still exploring, still testing the water—then we push them into the deep end of the pool, and the challenges described earlier lead to anxiety and doubt. *Is this really for me? Can I do it? How can I know?* To some extent, this is to be expected; professional development is an ongoing and typically nonlinear process of growth. How trainees fare clinically at the beginning of their practicum is at best an imperfect indicator of how they will fare at the end, let alone after years of being a licensed practitioner. Some uncertainty is a necessary and predictable part of the process.

22. McAdams, *Stories We Live By*, 39–65.
23. McAdams, *Stories We Live By*, 73.

Even so, it helps to keep in mind the well-known distinction between *primary* and *secondary callings*. In everyday speech, even among Christians, it has become common to speak of our "calling" or "vocation" in mostly secular terms, as a synonym for "job," albeit with a vague, superadded sense of transcendent purpose. But "calling" implies a personal act by which we are called by or to someone, just as Jesus called the Twelve to follow him. Thus, as Os Guinness insists, "Our primary calling as followers of Christ is by him, to him, and for him. First and foremost, we are called to Someone (God), not to something . . . or to somewhere."[24] We may then have one or more secondary callings in response to the primary call; one might say that both how we live and what we do for a living are meant to embody that response. As Ben Witherington has written:

> In terms of vocation, every Christian has a primary obligation to fulfill the Great Commandment and the Great Commission. . . . There are secondary callings we may be called to in addition to this—being doctors, lawyers, businesspeople, ministers, parents, etc. But they are indeed secondary callings. Our primary task as persons recreated in the image of Christ is to do the very thing Christ came to earth to do—share the Good News of salvation, healing, the coming of the kingdom. There are a variety of ways, venues, and avenues for accomplishing the primary task, and it can be accomplished in tandem with and even by means of the secondary callings or tasks.[25]

Historically, however, the ongoing challenge has been to hold the primary and secondary senses of our vocation together, and to keep first things first.[26] Guinness notes two typical ways of distorting the relationship between the primary and secondary. The first is the one suggested earlier: "vocation" is understood in a way that minimizes the direct relevance of the God who calls,

24. Guinness, *Call*, 31.
25. Witherington, *Work*, 46.
26. Guinness, *Call*, 31.

with the result that the word becomes barely distinct from "job" or "occupation." The second and opposite error is to over-spiritualize the language of "calling," such that only people who pursue full-time ministry are said to have a calling from God, robbing other pursuits of a sacred dimension.[27]

To these I would add a third distortion, which I suspect is quite common among contemporary evangelicals: believing that God calls us into one specific form of service or career, which we must discover if we want God's blessing. It's something like a career-oriented version of the romantic ideal of having a soul mate: *Somewhere out there is the one person God has chosen for you from the beginning of time!* Applied to our sense of vocation, such a distortion conflates our primary and secondary callings in a way that often leads to anxiety and shame for those who are still in the process of exploring. Against such distortions, a Christian sense of vocation must preserve the distinction between its primary and secondary aspects, and both must be rightly ordered in relation to each other.[28]

Put differently, the life story of anyone who claims to follow Christ must have a substantively transcendent dimension, by which personal narratives are embedded within a larger biblical metanarrative.[29] In terms of our tacit theological training, I fear that the gospel is too often presented in such a way that makes this difficult by getting the message the wrong way around. Often, the message is, "You have a problem, and Jesus is the answer." While

27. Guinness calls these the "Protestant distortion" and the "Catholic distortion," respectively (*Call*, 31–42). In my experience, Protestants are guilty of both.

28. Mark Labberton writes: "If we embrace and practice our primary calling to live as followers of Jesus in the most practical and ordinary contexts of our lives, the meaning of our secondary call will more likely occupy its appropriate place and will bear the weight and priority that is formed by what matters most" (*Called*, 169).

29. Many theorists who write from narrative perspectives, including narrative therapists, would explicitly reject the idea of subjecting our personal narratives to the authority of externally derived metanarratives, on the basis of postmodern assumptions. See, however, my argument in Lee, "Agency and Purpose in Narrative Therapy."

there is obviously some truth to that way of putting the good news, it risks reinforcing the tendency toward a kind of theological narcissism. We see God as a character in our stories—albeit an important one!—without a corresponding ability to imagine how *we* might be characters in *God's* story.

The primary and secondary aspects of our vocation, in other words, are not on the same logical footing; the first stands in a meta-relationship to the second. Christians have great freedom of choice in pursuing their various secondary callings. But this should not be thought of as picking from (or agonizing over) a list of religiously acceptable careers. The question is not, "Is it okay for a Christian to be a therapist?" Nor is it, "Will God reject me if I don't make the right career choice?" The question is, "If I become a therapist, in what way can this embody my primary calling to do the work of Christ?" That way of thinking, I believe, can give us some vocational freedom and help us endure some of the growing pains and the intrinsic difficulty of the work.

Note that similar observations could be made about the decision to pursue vocational ministry. It's far too easy to assume that it would not only be acceptable but laudable for Christians to devote themselves full-time to congregational ministry or the mission field. It should never be taken for granted, however, that such a choice automatically means the fulfillment, without remainder, of our primary vocation. Our primary and secondary callings must be kept in right relationship to each other; they are not identical, even in the case of full-time ministry. Indeed, although I have no hard data on this, I suspect that many pastors over-identify their primary service to God with their secondary choice to serve a local congregation. They may then experience a crisis of meaning when the congregation doesn't seem to appreciate their gifts as much as they had hoped, and are left to wonder, *What was God thinking?*

But that's another discussion for another time.

AGENTS OF SHALOM

Around what theme, then, might we organize a coherent and integrated sense of vocation? The one I have used most consistently in recent years, the one I have found most compelling and fruitful, is *peacemaking*. I am not claiming that this is the only theme possible, nor that I reached this conclusion at the end of a long chain of logical deduction. But the choice has personal significance for me—so I need to tell you a story.

I think back to when I was probably about eleven or twelve years old; I can't be sure of the age. I was not a Christian and had not grown up in a Christian family. My only experience of church was when we visited my grandparents during the holidays and were forced to attend with them. I don't remember understanding anything of what went on there—like why the pastor, ever the showman, would occasionally break out in song in the middle of a sermon. The one thing I do remember is wondering why I couldn't just spend the quarter I was given to put in the offering plate.

For some reason, at that age I suddenly decided that it was time to get religious. My grandmother had given me a Bible: a little blue pocket-sized New Testament (with Psalms) from the Gideons. Not knowing what else to do, I decided to begin at the beginning, with the Gospel of Matthew. The experience was less like reading a book and more like deciphering an ancient relic. The leatherette cover smelled musty, the pages were yellowed, and the text was King James. All those unpronounceable names in Matthew's genealogy, all those "begats": I was in trouble right from the beginning. The Christmas story, fortunately, at least sounded a bit familiar, so I persevered for a few more chapters.

And then I came to the Sermon on the Mount. It was like finding myself standing at the edge of the Grand Canyon; the vista was so vast and deep that I couldn't begin to take it all in. I knew next to nothing about Jesus. But these words—whatever they meant, I knew they had to be taken with utter seriousness, and so did the person who uttered them.

I had a problem, though, with the very first part of the sermon, those paradoxical, mysterious verses I would later come to know as the Beatitudes: "Blessed are the poor in spirit, for theirs is the kingdom of heaven" (Matt 5:3) and so on.[30] I was only a kid, but what Jesus was describing sounded nothing like any kind of blessing I knew: poverty of spirit, mourning, meekness, hunger and thirst. It was hardly an auspicious place for an eleven- or twelve-year-old middle-class American kid to start learning how to get religious, especially without any adult guidance.

It would be a few more years before I would become a believer, and many years more before I would circle back to actually study and write about Jesus' strange notion of blessing in the Beatitudes.[31] Jesus was sketching a countercultural portrait of the messianic kingdom that was "upside-down" from what most people expected—and from what we still expect today.[32] I'll say more about the Beatitudes over the next two chapters. For the moment, however, suffice it to say that I take these verses to have an inherent logic, and take the statement, "Blessed are the peacemakers, for they will be called children of God" (Matt 5:9), to be the culmination of that logic and thus a fitting theme around which to organize an understanding of our primary vocation. Let me therefore conclude this first chapter with a brief overview of how I understand the task and vocation of peacemaking.

Jesus was not, of course, introducing an entirely new idea. He quoted frequently from the prophecies of Isaiah, in which peace—or in Hebrew, *shalom*—was often cited as a sign of God's salvation in general and of the messianic age in particular (e.g., Isa 9:6–7; cf. also 26:1–3; 32:16–18; 52:7; 55:12; 57:18–19). The word is rich with meaning. I'm reminded of Cornelius Plantinga's memorable characterization of shalom as "the way things ought to be": "In the Bible, shalom means *universal flourishing, wholeness, and delight*—a rich state of affairs in which natural needs are

---

30. Unless otherwise noted, all Scripture references are quoted from the New Revised Standard Version.

31. Lee, *Unexpected Blessing*; Lee, *Marriage PATH.*

32. Kraybill, *Upside-Down Kingdom.*

satisfied and natural gifts fruitfully employed, a state of affairs that inspires joyful wonder as its Creator and Savior opens doors and welcomes the creatures in whom he delights."[33] Consider the creation story in Genesis 1. Six times as the narrative proceeds, God looks at what he has created and sees that it is good (vv. 4, 10, 12, 18, 21, 25); at the end of the sixth day, he looks back over all that he has created, and sees that it is very good (vs. 31). That's my picture of shalom: it's the way things ought to be, the way things were created to be, coming from the hand of a loving and gracious God.

Perhaps that sounds like too grand of an abstraction. But Plantinga speaks of shalom in a way that includes the satisfaction of "natural needs." Indeed, as used in the Old Testament, the word encompasses an ordinary sense of physical well-being. In Genesis 37:14, for example, we read that Jacob sends his son Joseph to see "if it is well" with his brothers; in 1 Samuel 17:18, Jesse sends David to see "how [his] brothers fare," because they have followed Saul into battle against the Philistines; in Psalm 38:3, the psalmist complains, "there is no health in my bones because of my sin." In each case, the word used to indicate some aspect of well-being is *shalom*.[34] Taking it further, when God promises a covenant blessing of shalom to his people, he does so in terms that would resonate with their way of life, naming things for which they would naturally long: the gift of rain and a plentiful harvest; a sense of safety that allows them to sleep peacefully; the removal of hunger, fear, and shame (Ezek 34:25–30).

In the contemporary world, we most often think of peace as the absence of conflict. But that is only one expression of a far richer biblical concept of peace. More than the mere absence of negative things like fear or hunger, peace as shalom is the presence of positive things like health and wholeness, safety and prosperity, all ultimately in a context of justice in the relationships between people and nations. When I teach this concept to couples, I ask them to imagine Genesis 1, and the pleasure of God at the

---

33. Plantinga, *Not the Way It's Supposed to Be*, 10; italics in original. Sin, by contrast, is "culpable shalom-breaking" (14).

34. Yoder, *Shalom*, 11–13.

goodness of creation. Then I ask, "What would need to happen in your marriage for God to look at it and declare 'It is good'?" It might be as simple as a momentary truce between them, a cessation of hostilities. The more constructive side of shalom, however, might be found in their taking hold of some thread of hope for the future, their faltering but growing hunger to do what's right by God and for the marriage, or their commitment to cultivating the qualities of humility and compassion in their relationship.[35] All of these, the absence of the negative and presence of the positive, are examples of the real-world, human embodiment of shalom.

My proposal, again, is that at least part of the need for integration stems from problems of narrative coherence, and that the related ideas of shalom and peacemaking can provide the thematic basis for an integrated understanding of our vocation. As Perry Yoder has written, shalom is "a powerful symbol of God's purpose and will for our world."[36] For therapists to be peacemakers may include helping people to resolve conflict, but extends far beyond. Peacemaking requires a robustly eschatological vision, which in turn means cultivating the ability to imagine our secondary callings as taken up into the redemptive purposes of God. It is God who desires shalom for a creation spoiled by sin, and it is God who by grace calls us to be agents of that shalom.

I think here of what I suspect may be the most widely cited passage from the prophecy of Jeremiah: "For surely I know the plans I have for you, says the LORD, plans for your welfare and not for harm, to give you a future with hope. Then when you call upon me and come and pray to me, I will hear you. When you search for me, you will find me; if you seek me with all your heart" (Jer 29:11–13). I have heard Jeremiah 29:11 cited routinely in sermons and in conversations between Christians; significantly, the word

---

35. Lee, *Marriage PATH*, chapters 2–8. This also points to the discussion of what I will call the "clinical virtues" of hope, humility, and compassion in the next two chapters. See also Strawn and Hammer, "Spiritual Formation through Direction."

36. Yoder, *Shalom*, 18.

that the New Revised Standard here translates as "welfare" is *shalom*. God's plan for his people, in other words, is peace.

Unfortunately, the verse is often used in a theologically narcissistic way. The message conveyed is that if we would just keep the faith, keep praying, and keep waiting, God will fix whatever is problematic in our stories. When verses 12 and 13 are added, it's often in the context of calling the embattled American church to pray diligently for God's help to survive and thrive in the midst of a godless society.

But seldom is the famed eleventh verse quoted together with the verse that immediately proceeds it: "For thus says the LORD: Only when Babylon's seventy years are completed will I visit you, and I will fulfill to you my promise and bring you back to this place" (Jer 29:10). The problem is that the idea of waiting seventy years rubs our tacit theology the wrong way. We'd rather take hold of God's promise of peace right now by making it the happy ending to the dramatic tensions of our own life stories. Jeremiah, however, will have none of it. The promise will be kept, but on God's eschatological calendar, not ours.

Meanwhile, what? If verse 10 too often goes unaccounted for, so does verse 7: "But seek the welfare of the city where I have sent you into exile, and pray to the LORD on its behalf, for in its welfare you will find your welfare" (Jer 29:7). *Seek the shalom of the city,* says God through the prophet, *for in its shalom you will find your shalom.* Walter Brueggemann comments:

> Imagine that! A letter written to displaced persons in hated Babylon. . . . And the speaker for the vision dares to say, "Your *shalom* will be found in Babylon's *shalom.*" The well-being of the chosen ones is tied to the well-being of that hated metropolis, which the chosen people fear and resent. . . . Depending on how deep the hatred and how great the fear, this promise of *shalom* with hated Babylon is a glorious promise or a sobering thought; but it is our best vision, a vision always rooted in and addressed to historical realities.[37]

37. Brueggemann, *Peace,* 22; italics in original.

Centuries later, the apostle Peter, writing to scattered and persecuted Christians, would also address them as "exiles" (1 Pet 1:1; 2:11). He instructed them never to repay evil or abuse in kind, but to repay with blessing instead, because they were called to be a people who pursue peace, that they "might inherit a blessing" (3:9–11).[38] Exiles seek a comprehensive and relational peace, and in so doing, find their shalom.

I don't know how often or how deeply we here think of ourselves as exiles. There's a broad spectrum of the amount and type of displacement and marginalization each of us has experienced. If the truth be told, some of us pray for revival in Babylon without recognizing the extent to which we have tacitly become Babylonians ourselves. We may not approve of everything about the culture in which we live, but we may feel very much at home here, thank you very much.

Yet we are called to actively seek the shalom of the city. That, I believe, is one way to frame, thematically, the primary vocation of a Christian therapist. The mental health needs of our communities—and dare we say it, of our churches—are great. In and through our secondary vocations as psychotherapists or those who in some way support the provision of mental health services, we engage our primary calling to be peacemakers, agents of shalom.

This calling, of course, is not unique to therapists. But it may be particularly important for Christian therapists and therapists-in-training to understand, for they will have direct influence over the lives of others and train in contexts that often undermine their narrative coherence. We need to get the story of our primary calling straight before considering its secondary expressions. We must first begin to take hold of our identity as those who have been called to participate in God's work of shalom-making; only then can we ask coherently how peacemaking might be expressed in the relationship between therapist and client. That will be the subject of the next two chapters.

---

38. The word translated "peace" is the Greek *eirene*, which in New Testament usage picks up the meaning of *shalom* and links it theologically with the good news of what God has done in Christ. See Yoder, *Shalom*, 9–21.

RESPONSE

Terry D. Hargrave

Be it fortunate or unfortunate, Cameron Lee and I share a love for old movie musicals. As I read Cameron's excellent and compelling paper on integration, integrity, and peacemaking as vocation, I was taken with the idea that theological and psychological education often results in "rocking the boat" of those who participate in the endeavor. I could not help but think of Stubby Kaye singing in the movie version of *Guys and Dolls*, his "Nicely Nicely" version of *Sit Down, You're Rockin' the Boat*. In that spirit, I would add my advice to Cameron:

> The people all said sit down, sit down you're rockin' the boat.
> The people all said sit down, sit down you're rockin' the boat.
> And the devil will drag you under, by the sharp lapels of your checkered coat.
> Sit down, sit down, sit down, sit down, sit down you're rockin' the boat.

Cameron Lee is a boat rocker by nature and it is a worthy endeavor to explore this important tenet of integration. My hope is that he will never stop rocking the boat in this area of spirituality and science.

I appreciated the meticulous way Cameron points out what integration means and the differentiation between an inter-disciplinary integration versus an intra-disciplinary integration. As he states it, bringing the X and Y together in a coherent whole is more difficult than just having psychology and theology as distinct and whole disciplines in themselves. When I read his reference to the X and Y, I immediately thought of this wholeness or newness that comes together when the X and Y meet in procreation and what is required of the two people to yield a brand new human being. I most often think of this formation of a new and coherent whole in terms of human couples creating a third identity in relationship called "us."[1]

First, procreation requires the two humans to lose a good portion of the "stuff" that makes them who they are in terms of preferences, personalities, and goals. When the gametes from a couple meet, they both represent exactly half of the original genetic code. Secondly, and perhaps even more germane here, as the gametes come together to complete the new genetic code, there is a randomness of coming together. We did not receive the best traits from both of our parents; indeed, we received a seemingly random part of their traits. For me, this is the amazing part of conception. The new human is *like* both parents because he or she shares the genetic information, but in reality, he or she is a totally *new* human being unlike any person that has come before or will come after. I believe it is a real testimony of a couple's struggle to become intimate with one another that what is produced and is the fruition of sexual intimacy—perhaps the most intimate thing we partake in as humans—is the creation of a whole new person and identity. My wife and I each think of our children not as *my* son or daughter, but as the physical representations of our "us-ness" or what we are together.

I think this holds guidance for us when we consider the integration of theology and psychology. When the X and Y meet in the relational interaction of integration, they by definition lose part of their identities or the specifics that individually make them each coherent fields of study. In a very real sense, when we integrate psychology and theology, we create a whole new field of endeavor—one that has its own identity, foundations, and methodologies.

1. Hargrave, *Essential Humility of Marriage*.

Yes, the new integration or coherent whole has likenesses toward both psychology and theology, but it is definitely its own field and will produce new ways of thinking that are very different from both of the parental disciplines. Like procreation and the creation of the third identity, we do not have a picture of this puzzle that represents the new field, so it must be random by creation. Neither field can bring all of its pieces to the table. I like that Cameron challenges us in this way that the process of integration is not predetermined and is by nature messy and unpredictable. If I read between the lines, where we would normally be frightened of this messiness and retreat back to our respective fields, he encourages us to move forward in this intellectual and emotional procreative act, trusting that what we will yield will be a testimony of the "us" that exists between psychology and theology.

It bears reminding us that this is a good thing. Like science and art—which in my mind both seek beauty and truth—each explains and illuminates things the other cannot. Science can tell us about and measure the physiological changes when a person encounters their beloved, but it is the poet who can express it thus: "This love of ours is as fresh as a morning glory, kissed by the dew, and in harmony, it rides with the timeless chariot's turn."[2]

As I mentioned, I love the idea that integration and education rock the boat. Integrity, as Cameron explains, is based in trust, consistency, and reliability. But the wild card here—and it is a very powerful wild card—is that all this personhood and integration takes place in the context of learning. Challenging what has always been thought or the presuppositions one carries is at the crux of learning. This is where we hit the truly inter-disciplinary nature of integration: a coming together of not just the psychological and theological, but both disciplines being integrated as a whole by a learning and growing human being, who is becoming more human as a result of deeper learning. Cameron clearly points this out by noting that as we do the work of integration, lectures are provocative and often destabilizing. It is destabilizing because it is meant to be destabilizing. It is essential in development and

2. Maiz, "This Love of Ours."

growth. However, it is essential to point out that Cameron's "boat rocking" does not carry with it the purpose of capsizing the personhood of the individual, nor depriving him or her of any part of the consistency of call and value in the midst of growth. Integration with integrity always points us toward developing, but not toward the chaos of losing self. This process of constructing and deconstructing through the process of learning is immensely and heuristically sound and one of the main aspects of Cameron's paper that points me toward his idea of integrity in this process of integration.

So now that we have explained the process and the goal, how do we go about the mechanics or engineering of integration? Here I like very much Cameron's diagram portraying the aspects of theological reflection and formation. It seems to me, however, that as helpful as the diagram is in terms of pointing out the differing influences, the reality is more patterned. We live and embody theology and psychology in the context of the corporate and then make sense individually of what it means. We can do it in the opposite sequence, but my point here is we usually do not, nor can we easily do it at the same time. It is more of a systemic sequence than the diagram suggests. In other words, our corporate interactions with the other tend to challenge and grow everything that we are as individuals. As we as individuals grow and change, the nature of our corporate interactions expands and changes. The same is true with the focal and subsidiary awareness. Developmentally, we most often have to learn from the focal to command the process and only then can it move to the subsidiary. We do need both, but it is more patterned than happening simultaneously. I believe this pattern really systemically only makes sense in the context of repeated interaction or practice. For instance, Cameron points out the focus needed to use a hammer to drive a nail. In his example, even though our focus is on the head of the nail, we are aware of the subsidiary details of the feel, heft, and balance of the hammer. While this is true, the process of learning those subsidiary details of managing balance, weight, and motion only comes in the context of repetition and practice. After all, how many of us were successful in commanding all the details of balance, motion, and direction the first time we were on a bicycle?

Again, to illustrate the point, I very much appreciated the metaphor of the concert pianist. Yes, both forms of awareness—focal and subsidiary—must be in play, but the balance of the two is learned in a patterned way. First, heavily concentrating on the focal points of notes and rhythm and then as more growth and familiarity takes place, subsidiary awareness. Many would say the real joy of a great performance is when the focal dimension is patterned into the subsidiary; the focal awareness of the artist then becomes the connection of performance, venue, and audience.

The real danger is if we do not engage these elements in a patterned way, it will not stop the challenges to our identities and senses of safety. And if we reject the other influences because we "already know what or how we believe," we lose the benefits of not only learning, but of integration. However, we also lose when we become unrecognizable to ourselves just because the world teaches us a particular way. Balance, therefore, seems essential in the model as well as developmentally patterned. Pattern in a causal, learning manner perpetuates balance and suggests more sound pedagogy. I believe that Cameron would support this patterned and practiced learning idea in integration, but I feel it is necessary to point it out here for the sake of clarity. One way we could all consider making our integration sounder pedagogically is to move into this natural developmental pattern, which promotes growth and lessens the chaos of moving all directions from the diagram at the same time.

One of the frameworks that struck me from Cameron's paper was the concept and description of "narrative coherence." He recounts the four types of narratives as *global coherence, biographical coherence, causal coherence,* and *thematic coherence.*[3] It felt to me that the four types of narratives were primarily individual in nature and not bent toward the corporate or communal. Particularly in terms of identity narratives, I feel more attention must be paid to the communal perspective and not just the experience with the

3. Habermas and Bluck, "Getting a Life."

communal. My community holds much of the narrative about my identity for which I am unaware or have forgotten. Like being driven by the place where I was born or being told about myself when I was a toddler by my caregivers, much of my narrative exists within my community and only can become a part of me cognitively as my community makes me known to myself. This is particularly true when it comes to vocation. Our communities have knowledge of us that we cannot or will not see, but shapes who we are if we will listen. My major professor, Glen Jennings, for example, helped me believe about myself what I could not see at the time, which resulted in me being more than I could have imagined. It is a process of pattern that forms narrative with integrity.

I like very much also how this is put into context in Cameron's section on how a life story of following Christ must have a transcendent dimension. This also seems to move effectively to an inter-disciplinary approach between psychology and theology. For instance, when the rich ruler asks Jesus about the important commandments, Jesus confirms the theological answer in line with our primary calling. However, Christ then turns the table and asks for a psychological commitment that entails both the primary and secondary vocation: "Sell all you have and come." I believe this is the kind of ultimate integrity of integration Cameron is pointing toward.

Finally, I like the idea that peace and peacemaking is not just absence of conflict or, by logic, absence of want. It is fulfilling and building life, love, and trustworthiness. Clearly it is more than just a choice of what not to do; it is a choice of peacemaking which requires life in the Spirit. I am reminded how Paul clearly states this choice in Romans 8:5–6.

I love the idea from Jeremiah of seeking the shalom of the city, for it is in the shalom of the city that we find our shalom. It strikes me this seeking the welfare of the city would have largely excluded a theological language. It was rather an integrative language that was economic, political, intellectual, and yes, psychological. Yet, it is clear from the perspective of the Jeremiah passage that seeking the shalom of the city was an inter-disciplinary endeavor where the integration was one of absolute integrity.

CHAPTER 2

HOPE AND HUMILITY AS CLINICAL VIRTUES

Not long ago, I invited a young couple to my home; I had been asked to meet with them by friends from church. The couple was struggling in their marriage. To them, divorce seemed like the only way to end the pain, or at least keep it from getting worse. I'll leave out, of course, the confidential details of the crisis. But part of the problem was that they were suffering alone; the issue that separated them from each other also separated them emotionally from their friends and family. They could go out with other couples, have fun, and pretend that everything was fine. But the evening would feel hollow. Family members were sympathetic but at a loss to know what to say. And the two spouses were too emotionally reactive to successfully express their pain to each other. Trying to do so only drove them further apart.

I was there for consultation and pastoral support, and only met with them twice. I listened carefully, then validated and normalized their suffering. I helped them structure some positive interaction into their relationship, and set some boundaries on the negativity, to help keep them from spiraling too easily into unnecessary fights. I gave them referrals to two local therapists, coached them on how to make the decision, and made them promise to follow up. Then I prayed with them. From my perspective, nothing I did was particularly remarkable. But even with such simple interventions, you could see the transformation in their demeanor. They didn't feel lost or alone anymore. There were things they could do to make a difference, and there were people they could talk to who would be calm, patient, and understanding.

At the end of our time together, I asked them if they had any questions for me. They had only one, perhaps the most important one: "Is there any hope for us?" They were asking for neither a Bible verse nor an objective clinical prognosis. They were taking the risk of believing that positive change might be possible, and wanted some personal reassurance that the marriage could survive. They trusted me, and needed to hear me say it.

"Yes, there is hope," I replied, and I meant it.

They brightened up, and we said goodbye.

After they left, I was of two minds. On the one hand, I felt privileged to have helped, to see the light of hope in their eyes. On the other hand, I couldn't help thinking about how many other people in our congregation were suffering alone while publicly putting a cheery Christian face on things. We in the church are called to be a community of hope. But we can also be remarkably intolerant of brokenness. We often prefer a tacit theology in which we act as if believers should already have triumphed over everything in Jesus, and anyone with persistent suffering just needs to get with the program. The very thought made me a little sad, and ironically, I found myself asking the same question I had just been asked: "Is there any hope for us?"

The answer, of course, is still yes—but given the challenges all of us continue to face in our congregations, I have to keep reminding myself that this is so.

VIRTUE IN THE CLINIC

In this chapter, I want to introduce the concept of *clinical virtue* that is part of how I teach integration and the vocation of peacemaking.

Hope is the first of two clinical virtues we will discuss, followed by humility; in the following chapter we will address two more, namely compassion and sabbath rest. When I say that these are "clinical" virtues, of course, I don't mean to imply that they're only to be found in the clinic. Quite the contrary: I regard each to be an embodiment of the vocation shared by *all* Christians to be agents of God's shalom. To speak of "clinical" virtues is therefore to suggest that each has a practical and clinically meaningful expression within the secondary vocational domain of psychotherapy.

There is quite a voluminous literature on virtue ethics that extends all the way back to Aristotle, and it would be impossible to survey that literature here even if I were competent to do so. It is worth noting, however, that in the field of bioethics, there has been an ongoing and vigorous debate between the proponents of opposing models.[1] To oversimplify for the sake of argument, the dominant view is the principle-based approach—often known as "principlism"—which privileges a small set of supposedly universal moral principles such as *beneficence* (working for the benefit of others), *non-maleficence* (doing no harm), *autonomy* (respecting others' right to self-determination) and *justice* (treating everyone fairly).[2] Principlist approaches tend to rely on case studies of moral quandaries, in which difficult medical decisions are to be justified by the way they balance and embody the principles and any related moral rules.

The alternative to principlism, on the other side, is a whole range of virtue- and character-based approaches that emphasize the importance of narrative.[3] These tend to treat each medical decision as a unique moral situation; the patient's stories and meanings are to be privileged over universal principles. If it can be said that principle-based approaches to bioethics ask "What shall I do?" in difficult moral situations, virtue and narrative approaches focus

1. E.g., Jecker et al., *Bioethics*.

2. Perhaps the best-known example of this principlist approach is Beauchamp and Childress, *Principles of Biomedical Ethics*.

3. A sampling can be found in Nelson, *Stories and Their Limits*.

more on the question of "Who must I be?"[4] I'm reminded here of the book *Being Mortal*, Atul Gawande's marvelous meditation on aging and mortality.[5] Gawande's case studies, including that of his own father's illness, present us with poignant and difficult questions. When it comes to making end-of-life medical decisions, which is more important—prolonging life or preserving the quality of life? Which should we privilege—supposedly universal principles governing medical practice and patient care, or the particularities of each patient's personal narrative and how they wish their stories to end?

And if you're the patient, what kind of person do you want your doctor to be?

Rita Charon, who specializes in both internal medicine and literature, writes of a patient who came to consult with her about his back pain:

> As his new internist, I tell him, I have to learn as much as I can about his health. Could he tell me whatever he thinks I should know about his situation? And then I do my best not to say a word, not to write in his chart, but to absorb all that he emits about his life and his health. I listen not only for the content of the narrative, but for its form. . . . I pay attention to the narrative's performance— the patient's gestures, expressions, body positions, tones of voice. After a few minutes, he stops talking and begins to weep. I ask him why he cries. He says, "No one has ever let me do this before."[6]

This scenario is radically different from what I observed when I took my mother to a pain specialist. During the clinical interview, he glanced at her but looked mostly at his computer screen; she faced him and tried in vain to make eye contact. He asked about symptoms; she tried to tell him the story of what it's like to be her, to live in a body wracked with chronic pain. He listened for the information he needed to formulate a diagnosis and a possible

4. Jordan and Meara, "Ethics and the Professional Practice of Psychologists."

5. Gawande, *Being Mortal*.

6. Charon, "Narrative and Medicine," 862.

treatment plan; she wanted to be heard and understood. Charon insists that physicians need *narrative competence*, the ability to hear and respond appropriately to patient stories.[7] Without this, they may make medical decisions that are ethically justifiable from a principlist standpoint, but at the cost of treating the patient as a cipher, as a nameless body of symptoms.

Many ethicists, of course, argue that the choice between principles and stories is not black-and-white, either-or. There are strengths to each approach, and each needs the other.[8] On the one hand, for example, we need principles to help safeguard minimal standards of care, to teach us what we are generally obligated or forbidden to do.[9] On the other hand, a respect for stories helps practitioners make treatment decisions that are most in line with a patient's own goals.

But it is not merely the patient's stories that matter. The debate between principle-based and narrative orientations is, after all, a debate over *professional* ethics. It's not just about the role that a client's narratives should play in treatment decisions; it's about the role that a therapist's narratives play in his or her own professional and moral formation, the narratives that make sense of our questions about the kind of people we must strive to be as practitioners. There is more to sound ethical practice than just the application of universal principles, as even the authors of what is arguably the best-known principle-based text in bioethics have recognized:

> What often matters most in the moral life is not adherence to moral rules, but having a reliable character, a good moral sense, and an appropriate emotional responsiveness. . . . Our feelings and concerns for others lead us to actions that cannot be reduced to merely following rules, and morality would be a cold and uninspiring

7. Charon describes narrative competence as that which "human beings use to absorb, interpret, and respond to stories" and which "enables the physician to practice medicine with empathy, reflection, professionalism, and trustworthiness" ("Narrative Medicine," 1897).

8. E.g., John D. Arras, "Nice Story, But So What?," 65–88; McCarthy, "Principlism or Narrative Ethics."

9. Radden and Sadler, "Character Virtues in Psychiatric Practice."

practice without appropriate sympathy, emotional re-
sponsiveness, excellence of character, and heartfelt ideals
that reach beyond principles and rules.[10]

To speak of the clinical virtues, then, is to speak of a therapist's
character and not just his or her technical expertise or ability to
apply ethical principles.

If you would, do a little thought experiment with me. Reflect
for a moment on the following question: can one be a successful
therapist without being a person of good character?

I would guess that many of you thought to yourselves, "Well,
it depends on what you mean by 'success.'" It's not difficult to imagine a therapist who is successful in a business sense, but ethically
challenged—for example, someone who fosters the dependency of
high-paying clients long past the point of being helpful. It would
be comforting to believe that all therapists of poor character would
eventually be weeded out by low demand, or that all morally upright therapists would be rewarded with financial success. But
that's not the world in which we live and work.

There are other ways we might consider a therapist to be successful, ways that come closer to what we usually mean by a "good"
and not merely a "successful" therapist. At a minimum, of course,
a good therapist must be technically competent. In our modernist
and instrumentalist ways of thinking, therapists must possess the
specialized knowledge and skills needed to be professional change
agents. Indeed, our textbooks are full of case studies demonstrating how Therapy A is superior to Therapy B, giving the impression
that all we need to be good and successful therapists is to learn the
right techniques.

That's true to an extent. But research on psychotherapy outcomes suggests that the specific strategies that make Therapy A
distinct from Therapy B explain only a small part of what makes

10. Beauchamp and Childress, *Principles of Biomedical Ethics*, 30. Similarly, Knapp and his colleagues propose an "acculturation model" of professional ethics. They use the term "integration" to refer to how therapists must
hold together professional rules and their own heritage of moral values and
concomitant virtues. Knapp et al., "Dark Side of Professional Ethics."

treatment effective.[11] Some scholars argue that the most important factors in predicting therapeutic outcome are instead the
ones shared in common across treatments, including the clients'
characteristics, such as their level of distress or degree of impair-
ment. Another well-researched common factor is the quality of
the therapeutic alliance, that is, of the working relationship estab-
lished between the therapist and client, with the contribution from
the therapist's side being of particular importance.[12] Such research
demands that we ask what personal qualities of the therapist might
be involved in good therapy, beyond technical expertise in theory-
specific interventions.

Most of us, I think, believe at least intuitively that a good therapist must also be a person of good character, even if it's not always
said aloud. Again, this is not merely a matter of rule-following; the
one who adheres to ethical codes only to avoid professional cen-
sure is not a good therapist. Nor is the one who considers the profession of psychotherapy to be nothing more than a decent source
of extrinsic rewards like income or social status. Rather, a good
therapist, to borrow a concept from Alasdair MacIntyre, pursues
the moral goods that are internal or intrinsic to the practice itself.[13]

As every clinician knows, psychotherapy can sometimes
be an emotionally grueling profession. What keeps therapists at
it, client after client, year after year? It's not for the extrinsic rewards alone, like money or status. It's for the intrinsic ones, the
rewards that are inseparable from the practice of therapy. To be a
good therapist, for example, requires continual self-scrutiny, and
at times, this may feel burdensome. But as Irvin Yalom insists, this
is also an "occupational privilege," because it means that the active
therapist is never stagnant, but always growing and evolving as a

11. One meta-analytic study, for example, examined component studies, in
which the effectiveness of various therapies was compared to that of the same
therapies with various theory-specific components removed. The researchers
found no difference. Ahn and Wampold, "Where Oh Where Are the Specific
Ingredients?"

12. E.g., Barber et al., "Alliance Predicts Patients' Outcome"; Baldwin et al.,
"Untangling the Alliance-Outcome Correlation."

13. MacIntyre, *After Virtue*, 181–203.

person.[14] As the authors of one study of therapists found, the vast majority of participants believed that their work had made them better and wiser people.[15] Though therapists may not experience such intrinsic rewards in every moment of every session, they and others in the helping professions are sustained by the occasional deep satisfaction of knowing they've made a significant difference in the life of a person who needed someone to walk with them through their suffering.[16]

Drawing even further from MacIntyre, we can conceive of virtue as "an acquired human quality the possession and exercise of which tends to enable us to achieve those goods which are internal to practices and the lack of which effectively prevents us from achieving any such goods."[17] Clinical virtues would then be those stable traits, habits, and dispositions that therapists would cultivate through the practice of psychotherapy itself, making it possible to experience the goods intrinsic to the practice. Many candidates for such clinical virtues have been suggested. If, for example, beneficence and autonomy are key ethical principles, then benevolence and respect for others would be the corresponding personal qualities.[18] To these, another theorist has added such worthy traits as prudence, perseverance, courage, public spiritedness—and yes, integrity, hope, and humility.[19]

Why, then, am I here considering only the four virtues mentioned—hope, humility, compassion, and sabbath rest—and not others? If one is to include hope, for example, why not the other theological virtues of faith and love? Or why not draw upon more comprehensive catalogs of virtues which are readily available?

14. Yalom, *Gift of Therapy*, 256–60.

15. Radeke and Mahoney, "Comparing the Personal Lives."

16. Skovholt and Trotter-Mathison, *Resilient Practitioner*, 9–17; they refer to these as "joy-of-practice reactions."

17. MacIntyre, *After Virtue*, 191.

18. Radden and Sadler, "Character Virtues in Psychiatric Practice." The theoretical question is the relationship between principles and virtues; are virtues derived from the principles, or the other way around?

19. May, "Virtues in a Professional Setting."

Within the field of positive psychology, for example, Martin Seligman and his colleagues pored over hundreds of texts from a diverse variety of sources—from Aristotle to Augustine, Buddha to Ben Franklin—in an attempt to identify and classify potentially universal virtues and character strengths. In this way they identified six core virtues: wisdom, courage, humanity, justice, temperance, and transcendence.[20] Each of these six, moreover, was conceived as a cluster of two or more supporting character strengths. In this scheme, hope, humility, and compassion are but three of twenty-four character strengths, and each is a route to one of the six virtues.[21]

All of this is valuable. My purpose, however, is to create neither a taxonomy of virtues nor a comprehensive model of ethical therapeutic practice. I am not claiming that the four clinical virtues are the only ones needed by or relevant to a Christian therapist. I am claiming, however, that a therapist's character depends in part on the narrative coherence of his or her sense of vocation. This is what I mean by integration as integrity. It is similar to what Blaine Fowers has called an "integrated life"; Fowers argues that virtue ethics can enrich the discipline of psychotherapy by helping therapists recognize the goods internal to the practice and their contribution to "a coherent, meaningful life."[22]

Moreover, MacIntyre insists that virtue is not merely about the goods internal to practices, but the *telos* of human life in general, by which moral acts are made intelligible by some overarching narrative.[23] As suggested in chapter 1, I believe peacemaking to be one such vocational narrative, and I believe that hope, humility, and compassion are intrinsic to the logic of peacemaking in Jesus' Beatitudes. Sabbath rest does not flow directly from

20. Seligman, *Authentic Happiness*, 125–33.

21. Seligman, *Authentic Happiness*, 134–61. Note that Seligman does not discuss compassion directly in this book, but in another; see Peterson and Seligman, *Character Strengths and Virtues*, especially 325–36.

22. Fowers, *Virtue and Psychology*, 56.

23. MacIntyre, *After Virtue*, 325–36. Similarly, Brody writes, "a narrative conception of a lived life is essential for making sense of the ethical concepts of virtue and character" (*Stories of Sickness*, 181).

those verses, but I include it because I believe that some form of sabbath-like practice—and not merely what is commonly known as "self-care"—is crucial if we are to have a right relationship to both our primary and secondary vocations. For the remainder of this chapter, therefore, our task is to examine the virtues of hope and humility, in order to see their relationship to the Beatitudes and to peacemaking and how they might function as specifically *clinical* virtues.

THE PSYCHOLOGY OF HOPE . . . AND BEYOND

The very notion of a telos to human existence already puts us in the territory of hope. The benefits of hope as a psychological trait have been studied extensively. The classic formulation of hope theory by Rick Snyder and his colleagues, for example, defines hopefulness as having "the will and the ways" with respect to personal goals.[24] "Will" refers to a sense of personal *agency*: the hopeful person believes that she can do things that will help achieve her goals. "Ways" refers to the perception of viable *pathways* to those goals. Both forms of cognitive appraisal work together. Note that this is not the same as unbridled optimism, nor a Pollyanna-like denial of challenges and obstacles. The truly hopeful person is realistic in assessing what it will take to reach a goal. But compared to the person who is low in hope, one who is hopeful believes that she will in fact attain her goals, and experiences a higher degree of motivation and positive emotion as she focuses on the possibility of success rather than gloomy expectations of failure.

You can see the increase of both agency and pathways thinking in the couple I described at the beginning of the chapter. At the end of our first meeting, I gave them a simple but highly structured homework assignment to give them a much-needed experience of positivity. I warned them not to go beyond what I had instructed them to do, lest they try to do too much too quickly, fail, and add to their discouragement. They followed my instructions and had a

24. Snyder et al., "Will and the Ways"; Snyder, "Hope Theory."

small victory—which paid an additional dividend in hope. When I met with them for the second and final time, they were much more ready to believe that they could do something to improve their marriage, and that consulting with a therapist would actually help.

Hope provides the motivation for tackling one's goals, and there is ample evidence that being more hopeful is associated with more successful outcomes. Children who are more hopeful, for example, feel more competent and have lower rates of depression; hopeful students are less likely to view failures as setbacks; hopeful track-and-field athletes perform better than their less hopeful peers, even after the differences in athletic ability have been factored out.[25] Shane Lopez and his colleagues have conducted meta-analyses of over one hundred studies of hope, and here is their conclusion:

> Other conditions being equal, hope leads to a 12 percent gain in academic performance, a 14 percent bump in workplace outcomes, and a 10 percent happiness boost for hopeful people. To put this in practical terms, a group of typical high-hope students scores a letter grade better on a final exam than their low-hope peers. A group of high-hope salespeople sells as much product in six days as their low-hope colleagues do in seven days. And high-hope people are just plain happier than their low-hope friends.[26]

Such research suggests the benefit of assessing people's level of hope, then coaching and encouraging them to set and take steps toward achievable goals. The agency dimension of hope seems to increase in the earlier stages of therapy, while pathways become clearer in later stages as clients learn and apply new cognitive and behavioral skills.[27]

---

25. These and other findings are summarized in Snyder et al., "Hope Theory."

26. Lopez, *Making Hope Happen*, 50–51.

27. Irving et al., "Relationship Between Hope and Outcomes."

Hopeful ways of thinking, in other words, can be cultivated through therapeutic means.[28] How do therapists do this? Hope can, of course, be an explicit topic of conversation; therapists can use the language of hope to help clients imagine how the past and present of their "hope story" might lead to a desired future.[29] But it can also be done implicitly, even if the word "hope" is never mentioned. Therapists can empathetically validate the client's feelings of hopelessness or point out resources the client has forgotten about or ignored.[30] They can recognize the strength it took for clients to seek help in the first place, and reframe it as a sign that they have the personal initiative needed to succeed in therapy.[31]

All of this points back to the common factors argument and the role of client expectancy: to what extent is the outcome of therapy tied to the client's expectations as to whether therapy will be helpful? Here, I'm reminded of how researchers are rethinking the nature and importance of placebo effects. In psychotherapy outcome research, the methodological gold-standard is the randomized clinical trial. Some participants are randomly assigned to the therapy condition being studied, while others are randomly assigned to alternative conditions, one of which is typically a no-treatment control group or a placebo. In the placebo condition, no active intervention is given, but participants may actually believe that what they are getting may help—as when people think they are receiving some new, experimental medication but are actually being given a sugar pill. In order for the actual therapy condition to be considered effective, it must outperform the placebo condition.

The logic of this experimental design makes sense, but at the same time betrays an underlying bias as to the nature of what counts as a "real" therapeutic intervention or cure. Again, in our instrumentalist way of thinking, the "real" treatment is the one the

28. E.g., Cheavens et al., "Hope Therapy in a Community Sample."

29. Larsen and Stege, "Hope-Focused Practices During Early Psychotherapy Sessions: Part II."

30. Larsen and Stege, "Hope-Focused Practices During Early Psychotherapy Sessions: Part I."

31. Swift and Derthick, "Increasing Hope."

therapist intends, while the participant's expectations are treated as a nuisance factor. That bias has been challenged by researchers who study the placebo effect as a variable of interest in its own right. It's not just about including some pharmacological decoy as a control condition anymore. It's about studying how changing the shape, size, or color of the pill might make a difference to the outcome—even if the pill is chemically inert. One science journalist summarizes some of the research:

> Big pills tend to be more effective than small ones. . . .
> Two pills at once work better than one. . . . Colored pills
> tend to work better than white ones, although which
> color is best depends upon the effect that you are trying
> to create. Blue tends to help sleep, whereas red is good
> for relieving pain. Green pills work best for anxiety. . . .
> There are cultural differences, however, emphasizing the
> point that any effects depend not on placebos themselves,
> but on *what they mean to us*. For example, although blue
> tablets generally make good placebo sleeping pills, they
> tend to have the opposite effect on Italian men—possibly
> because blue is the color of their national football team,
> so they find it arousing, not relaxing.[32]

What these and similar findings suggest is that the common factor of a client's expectations is indeed a legitimate and predictable part of what makes treatment effective.[33] Not every positive expectation is hopeful, at least in Snyder's sense of agency and pathways; a client may feel inspired to confidence by a therapist's manner before having any clear sense of the pathway to recovery. Nevertheless, it's fair to say that therapists should be conscious of the benefits of hope, and seek to foster it in their clients.

As a clinical virtue, however, hope is a character trait of the clinician rather than the client, and unfortunately, there has been far less research on the hopefulness of therapists. To be sure, many therapists are familiar with the experience of feeling hope-*less* in

---

32. Marchant, *Cure*, 29; emphasis added. Marchant is not just a journalist; she has a PhD in genetics and microbiology.

33. E.g., Dew and Bickman, "Client Expectancies about Therapy."

the face of their most difficult cases. One therapist, for example, wrote of her feelings of failure as a novice practicum student treating a dual-diagnosis borderline client with whom none of her colleagues wanted to work. She was filled with youthful enthusiasm and intent on saving the world "one client at a time"—but quickly found herself overinvolved and overwhelmed. Working with that client was like walking "a narrow precipice between two deep chasms":

> On one side was a well of boundless and naïve optimism that, given enough time and effort, I could help anyone. On the other side was a pit of cynicism and hopelessness, into which I sometimes tumbled after losing my footing. When I was in the pit, I felt powerless to do anything. In the middle was that elusive middle ground called reality, in which both extremes had a hint of truth to them.[34]

Snyder might say that this therapist sometimes lost both her sense of agency and of a pathway to success. She felt hopeless and flustered; the therapy floundered and eventually failed.

There is some empirical evidence that the therapist's own positive expectation of change is an important ingredient of therapy. In one recent study, researchers found that therapist expectations explained a little over 7 percent of the outcome, a small but significant percentage.[35] The authors of another study reported that even when client hope increased during therapy, it wasn't the client's hope that predicted the outcome—it was the therapist's.[36] More research is needed to understand how and why this is so, but such findings lend credence to the notion of hope as a clinically relevant virtue.

As theologian William May asks, however, what would be the "metaphysical horizon" of such hope?[37] May argues that people who are seeking release from suffering easily grant authority to

---

34. Quoted in Skovholt and Trotter-Mathison, *Resilient Practitioner,* 45–46.

35. Connor and Callahan, "Impact of Psychotherapist Expectations."

36. Coppock et al., "Relationship Between Therapist and Client."

37. May, "Virtues in a Professional Setting," 262.

helping professionals. In response, helpers are tempted either to play messiah or else to shield themselves from their clients' pain by hiding behind an emotionally-detached professionalism. What Christian practitioners in particular need is theological warrant for their own ongoing hope as they are confronted daily by the heartbreaking reality of human frailty and hopelessness.

May finds that warrant in the prophet Isaiah's description of God's suffering servant as (in the classic King James rendering) "a man of sorrows and acquainted with grief" (Isa 53:3). We don't have to play messiah, because we already have a Messiah who has suffered and died to give life to others. We don't have to protect ourselves from pain, because death itself is no longer to be feared. We are freed, in May's words, "to perform whatever acts of kindness and service [we] can and even to receive them from others, as a limited sign of a huge mercy which [our] own works have not produced."[38] As we shall see, I also find warrant for hope in the biblical metaphor of "the kingdom of God," which as Brueggemann has observed "stands at the center of the social imagination of Jesus."[39] The Beatitudes, I believe, are an excellent example of that vision and therefore of the metaphysical horizon of a Christian practitioner's hope.

I've been teaching an adult Bible class nearly every Sunday morning for over twenty years now. I usually avoid using too many theological terms because I've had folks who, having stared blankly at me for most of the lesson, come up afterwards and tell me that I shouldn't make things so complicated, because the only thing that really matters is that we love Jesus. And really, I understand the mentality. If things start sounding too academic, some people will "check out" mentally, and I don't want to confuse them unnecessarily.

There are, however, some theological terms that I've insisted everyone learn, and *eschatology*—the doctrine of "last things"— is one of them (I've even made them say the word with me out loud). I do this because I want them to notice how consistently

38. May, "Virtues in a Professional Setting," 264.

39. Brueggemann, *Hope Within History*, 22.

the biblical writers evaluate the present in terms of God's demonstrated faithfulness in the past, and their hope in God's continued faithfulness in the future. Such a biblically grounded hope is the counterargument to the theological narcissism I mentioned in chapter 1. The Christian life is not simply about enjoying a private relationship with God, nor about how God is merely a powerful, saving character in our individual stories. It is about cultivating the eschatological imagination needed for our stories to be caught up into the narrative of God's restoration of shalom to all of creation.

The Beatitudes help us do this. "Blessed are the poor in spirit," Jesus declared, "for theirs is the kingdom of heaven" (Matt 5:3). Blessed too are those who are persecuted for the sake of righteousness, for the kingdom is theirs as well (Matt 5:10). This is a present-tense reality: theirs *is* the kingdom.

How might one react to such a proclamation? On the one hand, for those accustomed to the world's ideas of success and even to a narcissistic theology of how God rewards nice or properly religious people, these are odd ways to talk about blessing. If we come to the gospel from a position of pride and privilege, Jesus' words about poverty of spirit and persecution will hardly sound like good news. The point is even sharper in the Gospel of Luke, where Jesus not only pronounced blessings upon those who were poor, hungry, weeping, and ostracized, but also pronounced corresponding woes on those who were rich, well-fed, laughing, and treated with respect (Luke 6:20–26). Some scholars read these words against the background assumptions of a culture of honor and shame; Jesus is giving honor to those who would typically be among the dishonored.[40] And let's face it: who among us even today would not rather be rich, full, happy, and respected? The Beatitudes seem to point to a kingdom which is upside-down from

40. E.g., Neyrey, *Honor and Shame in the Gospel of Matthew*, esp. 164–89. Neyrey argues for a narrow reading in which Jesus is addressing the situation of people who have been ostracized by their families and communities for becoming disciples.

the values and priorities even God's own people had come to take for granted from their cultural setting.[41]

On the other hand, if we come to the Beatitudes as people who are already poor in spirit, powerless, or marginalized, then suddenly Jesus' words become good news. Jesus is not preaching a program of religious self-improvement. He is bringing good news to those who need and want it most, announcing to the poor in spirit that the very kingdom is theirs. But not just any kingdom, and certainly not a worldly kingdom. What is given is the kingdom of *heaven*, or in the other Gospels, the kingdom of *God*—and the blessings Jesus describes are meant to tell us something about this God, this king. The poor in spirit don't somehow "deserve" the kingdom, nor have they earned it. Rather, they are blessed precisely because they have a king who graciously embraces them, who embodies the very essence of humility and compassion and calls his followers—rich or poor—to do the same.

For Christians, the virtue of hope is grounded in the faith that God's blessing of the poor in spirit, the mourning, and the like, is the sign of an eschatological promise: one day, there will be justice. One day, all unjust forms of exile will be at an end. The divine project of peace that is already underway will be complete, and all will be as it should be. Jesus invites his hearers to see the sufferings of the present in terms of the long view of biblical history: "Blessed are those who are persecuted for righteousness' sake, for theirs is the kingdom of heaven. Blessed are you when people revile you and persecute you and utter all kinds of evil against you falsely on my account. Rejoice and be glad, for your reward is great in heaven, for in the same way they persecuted the prophets who were before you" (Matt 5:10–12). Those who suffer persecution in the present for Jesus' sake are invited to look both to the future and to the past. *Rejoice, beloved, because your reward in heaven is great. Think about the prophets. Weren't they persecuted and dishonored in their lifetime? But aren't their names honored now?*[42] *That's why*

41. E.g., Kraybill, *Upside-Down Kingdom*.

42. E.g., the reading of Luke 6:22–23 in DeSilva, *Honor, Patronage, Kinship and Purity*, 67–68.

you should rejoice: your reward comes as part of a gloriously storied history that began long before you were born. Christian hope is a "living hope," the assurance that we have "an inheritance that is imperishable, undefiled, and unfading" waiting for us, being kept ready for us (1 Pet 1:4).

"Theirs is the kingdom of heaven," Jesus says, twice. These present-tense declarations bookend a string of future promises:

> Blessed are those who mourn, for they *will* be comforted.
>
> Blessed are the meek, for they *will* inherit the earth.
>
> Blessed are those who hunger and thirst for righteousness, for they *will* be filled.
>
> Blessed are the merciful, for they *will* receive mercy.
>
> Blessed are the pure in heart, for they *will* see God.
>
> Blessed are the peacemakers, for they *will* be called children of God. (Matt 5:4–9, emphasis added)

Thus hope, as a Christian virtue, lives in the historical space between "theirs is" and "they will." "Theirs is the kingdom": despite possible appearances to the contrary, we accept in faith that the kingdom is a present reality and that the God who cares about the plight of those who live with oppression and shame is indeed sovereign. Because of this, we can cultivate the vision needed to enjoy the glimpses of that truth that are afforded to us by the Spirit. And "they will": in faith, we joyously anticipate the kingdom's final, glorious consummation.

This is not mere optimism. Hope, to be biblical hope, is courageously clear-eyed and realistic about evil and suffering. And yet it dares to remember that under the sovereignty of God, slavery can lead to exodus, and crucifixion to resurrection. Hope cannot be divorced or shielded from the troubles of lived history, or it becomes something other than hope.[43]

---

43. This is, essentially, Brueggemann's argument in *Hope Within History*.

HOPE FOR THE HUMBLED

Hope as a clinical virtue is closely tied to humility. Again, Jesus describes those who are poor in spirit and meek, those who mourn, and those who hunger and thirst for righteousness as blessed. In Luke, it's those who are just plain poor—not those who are "poor in spirit"—who are blessed. It's those who are hungry, not hungry for righteousness or justice. It's those who weep, or are hated and excluded by others. Jesus is not teaching that it is morally superior to be lowly, oppressed, or marginalized. These people are not blessed because there is something intrinsically good, right, or desirable about being poor or hungry. They are blessed because the kingdom of God belongs to them, because they are the recipients of God's favor and eschatological promises. The proclamation of blessing is less about who they are than about who God is, and that proclamation is good news indeed. Small wonder that they flocked to Jesus in person.

Humility, I believe, is the proper response to this good news. One might say that Jesus is describing *humiliation*—the state of being humbled or brought low by one's life circumstances—rather than humility as a virtue or character strength *per se*. But the association is unavoidable, for both are characterized by lowliness. For many people the word "humility" thus has connotations of an undesirable weakness of character, and it is only with the advent of positive psychology that empirical interest in the possible benefits of humility has grown. Researchers, however, have taken pains to distance the concept of humility from stereotypical associations with lowliness. As Robert Emmons, for example, has written:

> Although humility is often equated in people's minds with low self-regard and tends to activate images of a stoop-shouldered, self-deprecating, weak-willed soul only too willing to yield to the wishes of others, in reality humility is the antithesis of this caricature. Humility is the realistic appraisal of one's strengths and weaknesses—neither overestimating nor underestimating them. To be humble is not to have a low opinion of oneself, it is to have an accurate opinion of oneself. It is the ability

to keep one's talents and accomplishments in perspective
. . . to have a sense of self-acceptance, and understanding
of one's imperfections, and to be free from arrogance and
low self-esteem.[44]

From a psychological point of view, having a habitually low opinion of oneself sounds more like character pathology than a character strength, and for that reason the idea of an "accurate" view of oneself—a view that includes both strengths and weaknesses—is preferable. But that doesn't answer all of the questions regarding the construct and its measurement. By what criteria, for example, should researchers measure the accuracy of people's self-concepts?[45] For that matter, some scholars worry over the problems that come with attempting to directly measure humility at all.[46] Do you ask people to rate their own humility? Do you ask them whether their friends think they're humble? Researchers are still working at untangling such methodological and conceptual knots.

Nevertheless, numerous studies have examined a variety of expressions of humility across a wide range of domains.[47] Some concept of humility seems necessary to our understanding of both personality and relational health. The creators of one recent theory, for example, have argued that the Five-Factor Model of personality that has been the standard in recent decades should be replaced with a six-factor model that includes a new domain they label *honesty-humility*, and the research looks promising.[48]

---

44. Emmons, *Psychology of Ultimate Concerns*, 171.

45. E.g., the Delphi study by Rowden et al., "Understanding Humility." The researchers proposed a definition of humility that included being able to see oneself and others "accurately," but the panel of experts recruited for the study found the criterion problematic. Alternatively, while Peterson and Seligman also include accuracy of self-perception in their definition of humility, they insist that this is "secondary" to the quality of non-defensiveness (*Character Strengths and Virtues*, 464).

46. E.g., Tangney, "Humility," 411–19.

47. For a thorough review of this work, see Worthington et al., *Handbook of Humility.*

48. This is the so-called "HEXACO" model, an acronym for the six factors

Humility also seems to be one of the traits that underlies positive change in relationships and relational therapy. As one research team has written, "humility influences the self in a variety of ways. It opens us up to be influenced, to accept responsibility, to forgive, it increases our willingness to admit to problems and consider ways to improve our relationships. Humility seems to help us look past our own egos and do so in a non-defensive and honest manner."[49]

My colleague Terry Hargrave, for example, has argued that when two individuals marry, a third and shared identity is created; whereas before there was "you" and "me," now there is "us." Humility in marriage entails each individual being willing to make sacrifices to keep "us" healthy.[50] This relational humility can be seen in the willingness of each spouse to respond positively to bids for emotional connection even when they're not finished being angry, or in their commitment to listen to each other and be affected or influenced by what they hear.[51] Few couples, if any, show up in a therapist's office asking for help in being more humble—but many therapists will implicitly work with them to increase their humility just the same.

In our personal relationships, then, it helps to be humble. But what about in our therapist-client relationships? Is there such a thing as a clinical virtue of humility? In some ways, the idea flies in the face of cultural values that assign worth and status to people with advanced degrees, important sounding titles, and social power over the lives of others. Again, to quote William May (with apologies for the inherently sexist language):

---

of Honesty-Humility, Emotionality, eXtraversion, Agreeableness, Conscientiousness, and Openness to experience. See Ashton and Lee, "Empirical, Theoretical, and Practical Advantages"; Ashton et al., "HEXACO." For the Five-Factor Model see, e.g., Costa and McCrae, "Five-Factor Model of Personality."

49. Rowden et al., "Understanding Humility," 386.

50. Hargrave, *Essential Humility of Marriage*.

51. E.g., Gottman, *Marriage Clinic*. Gottman, however, does not use the word humility in describing such dynamics.

One does not usually associate this virtue with professionals. Quite the contrary, long training and specialized knowledge set them apart and touch them with superiority. . . . The young professional identifies himself with his competence; he pretends to be a relatively self-sufficient monad, unspecified by human need, while others appear before him in their distress, exposing to them their illness, their crimes, their secrets, or their ignorance, for which the professional as doctor, lawyer, priest, or teacher offers remedy.[52]

There are, of course, those who have cautioned therapists against professional arrogance. Harlene Anderson, on the basis of thoroughly postmodern assumptions, has famously advocated that therapists adopt a "not knowing" stance by which they would stop taking their own expertise for granted and give greater authority to the client's knowledge instead, in the context of a fully collaborative conversation.[53] At first, the idea left many therapists wondering: *If I'm supposed to be "not-knowing," then in what way am I an expert at all? Why should I charge people money? And why did I spend all that money and time getting licensed?* Such doubts are understandable. But they also betray the modernist understanding of professional expertise that Anderson wants us to question.

It's not that specialized knowledge is unnecessary or unimportant. The question is how one holds that knowledge in the context of a relationship in which there is a built-in disparity of power. Therapy is not the impersonal application of technical skill. It is the creation and maintenance of a collaborative relationship of trust. On one side sits the client, who may already feel diminished but is required to be vulnerable for therapy to proceed. On the other side sits the therapist, who has a somewhat mysterious authority that is granted institutionally by the social construction of his or her professional role. Therapists have the power to influence the lives of others, and what they do with that power matters.

---

52. May, "Virtues in a Professional Setting," 264–65.
53. Anderson, *Conversation, Language, and Possibilities.*

Let's be honest. As people-helpers, we enjoy experiencing the fruit of our professional power. Yes, in part it's because we genuinely want to bring health and healing to others. We truly want to see positive change in their lives, to see hope and vitality restored. But our motives are not always or entirely other-directed and altruistic. We enjoy bringing order to chaos because we like feeling powerful. We like the sense of agency and accomplishment that comes with being, in Yalom's words, the "midwife to the birth of something new."[54] That can be a beautiful instance of peacemaking, worth celebrating.

Yet if the truth be told, our uses of power are not always for the good of the client. Haven't we ever jumped the gun on an intervention because we were tempted to be all-knowing, or wanted to work a little professional magic? Haven't we defended an interpretation that the client resisted because we needed to be right? Haven't we told stories that flirted with the violation of confidentiality because we wanted someone else to admire our brilliance or goodness? The list goes on. If you're a practicing therapist, I'm sure you could add your own examples.

Moreover, it's not just what therapists do with their power, but what they do when they feel powerless. As we'll discuss in the next chapter on compassion, clients don't always follow the script in which they're supposed to come as supplicants to learn from the therapist's wisdom. They don't submit meekly to the therapist's supposed expertise but push back instead. Or they seem to gratefully receive the therapist's advice and direction during sessions, and then week after week fail to follow that advice outside of sessions. The therapist may be left wondering, *Why are they coming? Do they really want to change, or do they just want a place to come and complain? Is it me? Am I incompetent? And heaven help me, how much longer before this session is over?*

Interventions don't always work as dramatically as they do in the textbooks; often, for a variety of reasons, they don't work at all. One research team, for example, examined therapeutic outcomes at a university counseling center over a period of six years, using

54. Yalom, *Gift of Therapy*, 258.

data collected on seventy-one therapists and over six thousand clients. They used the outcome data to separate therapists by their level of clinical success; not surprisingly, they found a significant difference between top-ranked and bottom-ranked therapists in terms of the percentage of their clients who improved, stayed the same, or actually deteriorated. But the actual percentages reported are sobering. Just under 28 percent of the clients of the bottom-ranked therapists improved or recovered in therapy; over 10 percent of them got worse. The numbers for the top-ranked therapists were, of course, better—but it was just under 44 percent of their clients who improved or recovered, while just over 5 percent deteriorated. Thus, in this study at least, roughly half of the clients of even the best therapists were left unchanged by therapy, and a few left therapy worse off than when they started.[55]

Are such numbers representative? In the 1950s and 60s, critics proclaimed loudly that the prevailing methods of psychotherapy were ineffective.[56] Their fiery rhetoric launched an ongoing debate and a torrent of research. Not surprisingly, estimated success rates vary from study to study. In 1980, researchers published a thorough meta-analysis of 475 studies and concluded that, "Psychotherapy is beneficial, consistently so and in many different ways."[57] The authors added, however, that the effects don't always last and the role of factors such as therapeutic orientation, treatment duration, and therapist experience make much less difference than one might expect.[58] Nevertheless, on the basis of more recent meta-analytic work, outcome researcher Michael Lambert declares that psychotherapy is indeed beneficial "across a range of treatments for a variety of disorders," estimating that roughly two-thirds of recipients will show improvement compared to those

55. Okiishi et al., "Analysis of Therapist Treatment Effects." Clinical outcomes were measured using the Outcome Questionnaire-45, a well-validated instrument designed for just such a purpose. See, e.g., Lambert, "Outcome in Psychotherapy."

56. Perhaps most famous among the early detractors is Eysenck, "Effects of Psychotherapy."

57. Smith et al., *Benefits of Psychotherapy*, 183.

58. Smith et al., *Benefits of Psychotherapy*, 184–89.

who do not receive treatment.[59] The research continues, with the hope that the field will grow in its understanding of how better to predict treatment success and failure, even while therapy is in progress. Meanwhile, however, the idea that a third or more of clients may not be helped is legitimate grounds for a bit of professional humility.

Let me stir the pot even more. Another research team asked 129 private practitioners to rate their clinical skills by giving themselves a percentile rank compared to other clinicians with similar training. They also asked participants to estimate what percentage of their clients improved, stayed the same, or deteriorated. The result? A fourth of the sample placed themselves in the ninetieth percentile or above; in other words, 25 percent of the participants thought of themselves as being in the top 10 percent of clinicians. On average, clinicians rated themselves as being in the eightieth percentile; nobody rated themselves as below average. Furthermore, over half of the clinicians surveyed said that 80 percent of their clients improved, including a fifth of the sample who believed that fully 90 percent of their clients improved; for the sample overall, the average estimate was over 77 percent.[60] Such estimates are obviously out of step with the success rates cited above. In part, this is surely because the therapists in the study were basing their numbers on their own biased memories rather than empirical evidence. But that in turn suggests the possibility of a Lake Wobegon effect: when it comes to rating their own skills and success rate, therapists—and surely other professionals as well—all want to see themselves as above average. This is fertile ground for the cultivation of humility as a corrective clinical virtue.

There are very real challenges to being a therapist, and limits to what a therapist can do. Nothing can completely take these away—not higher degrees, not more workshops, not even years of experience. Challenges and limitations need to be recognized and accepted, for they represent opportunities to grow and to

59. Lambert, "Outcome in Psychotherapy," 43. For another useful review of the literature, see the appendix entitled "Is Psychotherapy Effective?," 389–400.

60. Walfish et al., "Investigation of Self-Assessment Bias."

reexamine our self-perceptions and vocational narratives. The modernist understanding of what it means to be a professional is at best a partial truth. Yes, we do have power. We do have knowledge. But what narrative will help us hold our integrity together when we have to make sense of both our professional power and our powerlessness? What narrative will sustain us when the so-called "talking cure" seems to be more talking than cure?

Again, for therapists who follow Christ, I propose the over-arching metanarrative of peacemaking. We need the hope-filled eschatological imagination to see our work as being caught up into the ongoing restorative work of God. From that perspective, the percentage of people we've "cured" through expert intervention is not the sole measure of our work. We don't save humanity one client at a time; it is not our vocation to be anyone's messiah. Rather, those who are called to be peacemakers, whatever the long-term outcome of a case, can take joy in witnessing moments of shalom as they unfold. When clients truly listen instead of putting up walls, take responsibility for themselves instead of blaming others, or turn toward each other instead of away, therapists can catch a glimmer—albeit sometimes a fleeting one—of peace.

Clients may not come to therapy seeking to grow in humility, but in one way or another they have been humbled by life and are looking for hope. Do we have the imagination to see them as deeply loved by the God who champions the poor in spirit? I think here of Jesus' attitude toward children. His disciples, apparently, struggled a bit with pride and often jockeyed with one another to increase their sense of self-importance. At one point, Jesus sat a child in their midst and said, "Truly I tell you, unless you change and become like children, you will never enter the kingdom of heaven. Whoever becomes *humble* like this child is the greatest in the kingdom of heaven" (Matt 18:3–4, emphasis added).

In another episode, people were bringing their children to be blessed by Jesus, but the disciples tried to prevent them, as if to rebuke them for wasting the Master's time. To their surprise, Jesus actually became angry and publicly scolded them for their shortsightedness: "Let the little children come to me; do not stop them; for it is to such as these that the kingdom of God belongs. Truly I tell you, whoever does not receive the kingdom of God as a little child will never enter it" (Mark 10:14–15). Jesus had already told his disciples that the kingdom belonged to the poor in spirit. Almost as an enacted parable, he embraced and blessed children. Children aren't humble by choice; they cannot be said to display humility as a virtue. But Jesus in compassion loved them because of their powerlessness and vulnerability, demonstrating both the character of God and the nature of God's kingdom.

Many clinicians these days work from an attachment theory perspective, in which a client's current behavior is understood as stemming in part from how they experienced the emotional vulnerabilities of childhood. Even the most arrogant and troublesome of clients may be so for self-protective and defensive reasons; their lack of relational humility acts as a shield against feelings of humiliation. Can we bracket our own negative reactions to our clients' provocations and imagine them as the vulnerable children whom Jesus delighted to embrace and bless? What might change about our therapeutic stance if we did?

This is but one possible expression of humility as a clinical virtue. There are others, including the willingness to develop greater multicultural competence, to work collaboratively with other health professionals, to accept critical feedback from clients, and to recognize when outside consultation is needed.[61] For these reasons, Steve Sandage and his colleagues have suggested that therapists might receive the virtue of humility as a "gift," though it may be a gift that few deliberately want. What the authors mean is that missteps, ruptures, and disappointing outcomes in therapy can be viewed as opportunities to acknowledge one's limitations and grow in humility, and they are careful to remain theologically neutral in the way they say this.[62]

In speaking of humility as a clinical virtue, however, I have no wish to be theologically neutral. Again, the children Jesus blessed may not have had any choice about their vulnerability and

---

61. Paine et al., "Humility as a Psychotherapeutic Virtue."

62. Sandage et al., "Humility in Psychotherapy," 301–15.

low social status. They were not humble in the sense of possessing virtuous character, but in the sense of being humbled by their circumstances, by their place in society. Jesus gave the disciples a choice: *See this child? You must become like this. You're so concerned about personal greatness, and think of the kingdom in those terms. Other kingdoms may work that way, but not the kingdom of God.*

Once more: the pronouncement that the kingdom belongs to the poor in spirit is good news . . . to those who are poor in spirit. It may be bad news to anyone else, or at best, paradoxical news. Nobody wants powerlessness or shame, especially those who have been indoctrinated into a proud culture of professional competence and expertise. I submit that what we need in order to be empowered in the virtue of humility is the virtue of hope; the two go hand in hand. We can both celebrate our successes and humbly learn from our limits and failures when we understand that our work is being taken up into the peacemaking purposes of God and thereby sanctified.

The clinical virtue of hope is not a matter of naively believing that every client will get better, nor that every intervention will be effective. There are too many factors involved in any therapy outcome, many of which are outside our control. Our hope is not simply for the future of our clients, but for the future of all creation under the ministrations of a gracious, promise-keeping God. With such eschatological hope, we can cling less tightly to our own needs for power and significance. With such hope, we are better able to endure the ups and downs of clinical work as we continue to work for peace. So too will our clients be able to draw both comfort and confidence from our non-anxious and humble presence.

Or so we must hope.

RESPONSE

Pamela Ebstyne King

Like the first respondent, Dr. Terry Hargrave, I agree that Dr. Lee should keep "rocking the boat." I was a student of his back in the 1990s, and Cameron's a rocker. In fact, you may not know this, but he has a great admiration for Elvis, and on some occasions has been known to sing like "the King" (of rock and roll that is), and thus if I were to give this response a title, it would be "Boat House Rock" rather than "Jail House Rock"—because when I was a student, he rocked my boat.

The night before my first class with Cameron, I could not sleep. My restlessness had less to do with the hot, sultry July night in a "just-married-grad-student-can't-afford-air-conditioning-apartment," and more to do with the unconscious anticipation of the deep stirring of vocational waters in my life. Back in the summer of 1995, I was a naïve and optimistic theology student wandering into the wild waters of the School of Psychology (SOP)—for what I thought was going to be a two-unit, two-week summer elective. Little did I know that two decades later I would still be in the SOP, but now as faculty.

In Cameron's class, "Family Life Education," something unique happened. Through my focal awareness, I took notes, wrote papers, and gained understanding of how the church might form and nurture people. I was informed. But through my tacit awareness or subsidiary knowledge—I was *transformed*. I encountered a man with a coherent life narrative. Somehow in his way of being and teaching in the classroom, Cameron and God's Spirit stirred my imagination—not just about growth and development, but also about the concept I would later call *thriving*. Cameron's way of being engaged my senses and ignited my emotions to bring about devotion to this idea of thriving and enabling people to become all who God created them to be. I was inspired by the life and person before me, as I perspired to master the course content.

And now, I am honored to conspire with Cameron in this endeavor of integration. I appreciate his informative and inspirational words on the clinical virtues of hope and humility, his insight into the importance of virtues as the embodiment of the vocation shared by all Christians as agents of God's shalom, and the formative value of narrative coherence to this end. His weaving of perspectives from the gospel, virtue ethics, narrative, psychotherapy, and psychological science on hope and humility not only teach us about these virtues, but they invite us further into our own journey of habituating hope and humility as part of our identity as God's ambassadors on earth—whether in therapy rooms, congregations, classrooms, or otherwise.

That two-week intensive was like a stick of dynamite in my *narrative coherence*. At that time, as an MDiv student, I was on my way to ordination in the PCUSA, and thought I was taking a little pit stop as an "elective" in the School of Psychology. I would never have imagined that what I thought would be a small vocational detour served to reroute my whole vocational journey. I was eventually ordained in the PCUSA to a "ministry of equipping" as a faculty member in the School of Psychology and eventually installed in the Peter Benson Chair of Applied Developmental Science through which I have studied and taught on spirituality and thriving. I'm glad Cameron rocked my boat!

The following response reflects on how entwined the virtues of hope and humility are in the context of the Christian narrative and how these virtues are seminal to our primary vocation as a follower of Christ as well as the secondary vocations that we pursue professionally as God's ambassadors on earth. Hope and humility offer important perspectives on our own role in the story of the gospel of love, grace, redemption, and flourishing. Both within the Christian and secular worlds, hope and humility are usually not paired—unless listed alphabetically. Hope is often viewed as expansive and motivating, and humility as constricting and inhibiting. Within the context of the Christian narrative, however, hope and humility are deeply connected. Hope gives us a glimpse of the expansiveness of God's love, and humility provides an openness or gateway to active participation in God's love story.

Keeping with the analogy of boat rocking, I say, "Life, keep rocking our boats!" Although I am always mindful that we should be careful what we pray for, we can say this with confidence because as Christians, we have "hope as an anchor" (Heb 6:19). The winds and waters of life might blow and toss out boats around, but we can take heart. Meditating on Hebrews, I can say that our hope is anchored in:

> the Lord God almighty,
>
> whose purpose is unchanging, unswerving,
>
> and although we are undeserving,
>
> our hope is in God,
>
> whose son, Jesus, entered the Holy of Holies
>
> and became the high priest in the order of Melchizedek forever and ever.

This is no ordinary hope. This is biblical hope, cast in light of *telos*, the purpose for which God has created us[1]—to be agents of shalom. This is biblical hope informed by not just a coherent narrative, but the transcendent narrative, the story of good news, the Gospel, that gives meaning that far outweighs everyday optimism. Optimism is a positive outlook toward the future. Our hope is not just a cheerful, wake up on the right side of the bed, positive outlook. Our hope has eschatological meaning. Our hope has a

---

1. *Telos* is Greek for purpose, goal, or completion and has served as a theological orientation for my understanding of human purpose. See Balswick et al., *Reciprocating Self*; King, "Reciprocating Self."

guarantee in the future. The Beatitudes remind us that those who grieve will rejoice and that the meek in spirit will inherit the earth (Matt 5:1–12). Our hope is eschatological, meaning that biblical hope is real and tangible and experienced *now*—in the present moment, and directs us towards the future with promises of what is *yet to come*.

This kind of hope has eternal gravitas. In fact, it is imbued with such sacred meaning and power that such hope has orienting power on our lives. This hope is not just meaningful, like a sentimental Hallmark card, but serves as a source of ultimacy that is vivified by the Holy Spirit and moves us and draws us deeper into relationship with the source of hope, our Lord, our God.

This is a living hope. This hope is not just a principle, but is relational. This hope is understood through our beliefs, but the transformational aspect of this hope stems from the grace and confidence we experience in knowing and being known by God. This hope is not just theoretical, but it is covenantal. It is based in the blood of the New Covenant, in which God became human, in Jesus Christ, who lived and suffered amongst us, who died on the cross, descended into hell, and on the third day rose from the dead. This covenant guarantees that we can have hope that death, despair, and disparity will be overcome. Experiencing the love of God confirms and convicts us of these truths. Thus, if we aim to cultivate hope in our lives, we cannot solely base our hope on our beliefs, but must increase our capacity to know and be known by God. We need not just focal knowledge, but tacit knowing.

Our hope is relation. It is found through the grace and face of God. Living hope has more to do with experiencing the gaze of God and living in the grip of God, than with the grades you get studying about God. As we lean into our relationship with God, we experience this transformative hope and begin to understand our call as part of God's ongoing work in this world. When we understand our life's purpose as our role in God's ongoing story of crucifixion and resurrection—life, death, and new life—then we will realize not only that our hope is anchored in God and that we can live into that hope in a vivifying way full of possibility, but also that this transcendent perspective nurtures humility.

When we see our lives in light of the arc of the gospel, God's story of creation, fall, redemption, and flourishing, we gain an eternal perspective of our lives. Such a view not only offers hope, but it also nurtures humility, which allows us to be more open to the transformative love of God. As Cameron mentioned, one way psychologists understand humility is as seeing oneself rightly. When we view our lives as part of God's story, we see ourselves as a beloved son or daughter of God, who is completed in Christ, and who plays an active role in God's ongoing work in this world.

Humility is seeing oneself rightly, in the eyes of God, as God's beloved creation—fearfully and wonderfully made (Ps 139; that is the perspective of the Creator of the universe!). Humility involves knowing and embracing oneself as God's beloved. Humility does not mean degrading oneself. It does not mean discrediting oneself. Humility does not mean being a wimp. It also does not mean false modesty. I don't remember when or where, but I once heard someone quip that humility is not an astronaut saying, "Oh, I commute for a living." Humility is also not shame. It's not thinking you are no good. Conversely, it's not acting like you are no good, when you think you are hot stuff.

In fact, the Bible makes a big stink about being uniquely gifted with spiritual gifts, having a place in a body of believers, and being called into a royal priesthood. We are all that. You, reading this chapter, are all that.

We can celebrate who we are as God's beloved creations, but we are still humble because we might be *all that*, but we are not *all*. Christ is our all. As Christians we affirm that we are made in the Image of God, but Christ is the perfect image of God (Col 1:15). Thus, becoming like Christ is our *telos*, our purpose. This helps us keep proper perspective. As much as I want to say, "Lean in and celebrate who you are," I also exhort us to not find our fullness or completion in ourselves. In several places in the New Testament we are reminded that our fullness is in Christ. For example, Paul writes to the Colossians, "In Christ you have been brought to fullness" (Col 2:10). This fullness is not found through us or through our efforts. It is found in Christ, and somehow we participate or share in Christ's fullness. This sense of fullness is not "ate-enough-pizza-full," but more along the lines of having a sense of completion as in "all is well with my soul" peace. So, although we can celebrate who we are, we celebrate who we are in Christ.

In addition, humility also involves seeing ourselves called as Christ's ambassadors or agents of shalom. Through our salvation in Christ, we are not just saved *from* sin, but saved *for* active participation in God's ongoing work here on earth. This notion of being agents of shalom or peacemakers is a crucial part of our identity in Christ and central to humility. Such a kingdom perspective allows us to zoom in, so to speak, and relish that we are God's beloved creation, then zoom out and realize that we are part of God's much bigger plan. When we see ourselves as God's beloved on the journey to being conformed through and to Christ, and as God's ambassadors of love and mercy—then we will see ourselves rightly. In this way, humility is not about belittling or undervaluing ourselves, but it is a posture that allows us to see ourselves in God's sight, giving us the freedom to become more ourselves through and for God.

Hope and humility are crucial virtues as Christians and as clinicians. Eschatological hope compels us and propels us towards God's purposes for us. Humility enables us to realize that there is a story bigger than our own. In this way humility gives us the openness to go along with God's story and purposes. Humility allows us not to capitulate to the pressures of this world, but to trust that there is a way beyond our understanding and provides the willingness to trust, that God's "got this." Borrowing Snyder's description of hope, humility allows us to enter into, surrender to, and be swept up into God's "will and way."[2] In this way hope and humility build upon each other—both are responses to God's grace and purposes and both serve to entice and invite us into God's activities.

Hope and humility not only engage us, but sustain us in our fidelity to God. The power and encouragement inspired by hope,

2. Snyder et al., "Will and the Ways."

and the openness and surrender yielded by humility enable us to endure through both the calm and turbulent waters of life. Our humility before our Lord and God, Creator, Redeemer, and Sustainer allows us to sustain hope, even in those dark nights of the soul when it is hard to be confident that God is there. In the waiting for healing and restoration with a client or in our own relationships, our humility enables us to hold onto hope like a lifeline. And this lifeline is not adrift. Our hope is anchored in God, who does not go away and abandon. Our hope is anchored in the One who holds all of our life—the One who knows and sees and holds all of who we have been, are presently, and will become.

This hope is timely for those in the process of formation, for those who feel personally, spiritually, and/or vocationally under construction. Here I am speaking from experience. I mentioned how Cameron's two-unit class redirected my vocational journey, which two decades later seems coherent. However, there were many twists and turns, ups and downs, road bumps and potholes that did not always make for a smooth or clear ride.

This anchored hope is especially timely in an era marked by fragmentation, when the only thing constant is change, when so many are so disconnected and unmoored, when, just the night before the Integration Lectures, I had to talk about school shootings with my high-school-freshman son. When our times are characterized by a crisis of continuity, which results in a crisis of coherence and integrity. Such incongruence is evident in the disparity between what we post, and what we really are the most. In other words, this crisis of coherence is evident in the gap between the curated lives we offer on Instagram and Facebook and the disharmony we feel inside. These inconsistencies reflect our lack of intra- and interpersonal incongruence.

But as Christ followers, we can take heart—that all is well because our hope is anchored in God. I have been grateful, when the waters are turbulent and murky, that my hope is anchored in God even though I cannot see the anchor. I know that my lifeline is anchored to the God who does not go away and abandon. My hope is anchored in the One who knows and sees and holds all of who I have been, am presently, and will become.

In his profound little book, *Being Disciples*, Rowan Williams recounts Bonhoeffer's struggle to understand his own identity and conveys the poignancy of hope and humility.[3] In a poem, titled "Who am I?" Bonhoeffer writes:

> Who am I? They often tell me
> I stepped from my cell's confinement
> calmly, cheerfully, firmly,
> like a Squire from his country-house.

> Who am I? They often tell me
> I used to speak to my warders
> freely and friendly and clearly,
> as though it were mine to command.

> Who am I? They also tell me
> I bore the days of misfortune
> equally, smilingly, proudly,
> like one accustomed to win . . .

> Am I then really all that which other men tell of?
> Or am I only what I myself know of myself?
> Restless and longing and sick, like a bird in a cage,
> struggling for breath, as though hands were compressing my
> throat . . .
> weary and empty at praying, at thinking, at making,
> faint, and ready to say farewell to it all?

Bonhoeffer goes onto ask: "Who am I? This or the other? Who am I? They mock me, these lonely questions of mine." He concludes: "Whoever I am, Thou knowest, O God, I am Thine!"[4]

Even when we do not have the eyes to see our own lives clearly, God does. Humility enables us to admit that we may not have a full grip on our lives, and allows us surrender our lives to

---

3. Williams, *Being Disciples*.
4. Bonhoeffer, *Letters and Papers from Prison*, 347–48.

God's grip. We can all say with Bonhoeffer, "I am Thine!" In humility, we can know that our hope is anchored in the One who knows and sees and holds all of who we have been, are presently, and will become.

Just like an anchor holds a boat in place, God's holding our whole lifeline.

Bonhoeffer's words illustrate how humility gives way to hope, even when our lives feel like they are composed of several shredded strands, or our lives feel like they are unraveling, or that they have never fully held as a complete whole; when we can't hold our lives together or when lists on sticky notes can't hold us together; when we can't put our clients' lives back together. When the comings and goings—the ethnic, racial, religious, political divisions—all pull us in disparate ways, humility enables us to have hope and know that the God whose purposes do not change, holds all things, holds onto us, holds onto our clients, and we are all anchored in him.

I confess there are times when I feel like I can't hold on, and in those very humbling moments I am relegated to the confidence that God is holding onto me. In Williams' profound words, "I can be held when I don't feel I can hold on."[5] Such hope is initiated and sustained by God's faithfulness not my own. Sometimes the jarring confrontation of our own limitations—of not even being able to hold on by a shred or a thread thrusts us into an involuntary state of humility, and that is when hope breaks in as we realize that our faith has more to do with being held by the Master than our own efforts to master life.

Such hope is so much more than optimism or a positive outlook, so much more than mere confidence in the future. These are the variables many social scientists study in a reductionistic manner. Our hope is not reducible, it is irrepressible. It is deeply anchored in the God who does not let go. The God who's got you. No matter what. Even when your story is not coherent, when it doesn't make sense, when it is forever disrupted and altered by trauma, by school shootings, by a health crisis, or by relational devastation. You can trust that God's got you.

5. Williams, *Being Disciples*, 26.

Even when life is breathtaking—not in its beauty, but in its pain and desolation—we can have hope that God will redeem this pain. As peacemakers in this world, we can be stewards of this pain,[6] and care and lead others from within the depths of our sorrow and the depths of our deep hope.

This understanding of hope is an absolute antidote to the narcissistic theology that Cameron mentioned—a theology that places God as a supporting role in our own story. Hope casts light on God as the leading role, the director, the producer, editor, etc. as the Creator, Redeemer, and Sustainer, and humility gives us perspective to know our role in God's grand, amazing, unfolding story, and this is reassuring when we are on the journey of vocation formation. Even when we don't know who we are or who we are becoming, we can know that we are held onto and woven into God's unfolding tapestry.

Not only is this hopeful for those of us on the journey of vocational and spiritual formation, but just as our faith draws us into deeper hope and humility and offers a fuller view of how we might serve others in our secondary vocations as therapists, pastors, teachers, or otherwise. We offer them humility and hope through our words and our being. We serve to witness to the truth of their lives that they sometimes cannot see. As peacemakers our call is:

- To experience and reflect the dignity of each person—to see and behold their individual beauty. Such interactions serve to tacitly ignite the other to become more fully the person they were created to be;

- To invite people to envision God's greater reality and guide them to discover how they are part of God's story;

- To point or nudge others into fuller and deeper expressions of themselves as they connect and engage in deeper and more meaningful ways with God, others, and the world around them.

---

6. Buechner writes about being a steward of pain in his essay, "Adolescence and the Stewardship of Pain." See Buechner, *Clown in the Belfry.*

We can inspire our clients and those we serve by embodying God's hope; by presenting the broader, sweeping landscape of a bigger picture than what they can see; and by helping weave them into the fibers of the tapestry of life. This is beyond focal knowledge, but we must encourage them to cultivate tacit knowledge by encouraging them to feel, taste, hear, and see the textures of life by relating to them and engaging the senses of their humanity in a way that vivifies them and enables them to see themselves in God's light and woven into God's eternal tapestry.

Cameron's raising of the distinction between focal and tacit awareness is extremely important and timely. We cannot rely solely on intelligence—especially when the US media so often portrays Christendom as Christian-dumb! As Christians we need to not just rely on clever systems of knowledge; intelligence, science, and PowerPoint can only take us so far. Instead, we need to emphasize what Rowan Williams calls "dependable relation"; "in the dark night of the intelligence we are being nudged in the direction of understanding faith afresh in terms of dependable relations."[7] As therapists or ministers we can be those dependable relationships for others, through which those we serve are drawn into hope by God's Spirit. Core to our call as Christians is a summons to embody hope and to offer it to those we serve. The manner in which we do so is informed by our profession and our personality. In this way, we can provide anchors for those around us, always pointing them toward ultimate moorings in Christ.

In closing, I'll reemphasize that as Christians, we don't just have hope in principle; we have hope in relationship. We do not have mere theoretical hope, but covenantal hope. In order to live into our call as peacemakers, we must engage in practices that cultivate our capacity for knowing God, not in principle, but through relationship. We are called to be God's hopeful presence to others as peacemakers—whether in therapy or in the congregation or in school or in the marketplace. We embody hope through our humility, conviction, and experience of God's hope through God's grace. Through our words we can inform and educate on hope and

---

7. See Williams, *Being Disciples*, 27.

humility; but through our ways of relating and being, we tacitly form and impart hope.

I am grateful to Cameron and to so many other faculty colleagues whom I have had the privilege to know and be known by, who have been anchors of my own hope, who have explicitly and implicitly infused hope into my life. I'll counter Terry by saying, "Don't sit down, don't sit down, don't sit down . . . Keep rocking the boat!"

And to the rest of you, I'll say "Rock on!"

CHAPTER 3

COMPASSION AND
SABBATH REST
AS CLINICAL VIRTUES

As I write this, I'm thinking about this past Christmas. Specifically, I'm thinking about Christmas cards. My wife and I receive very few of the traditional style of cards anymore, the ones adorned with colorful, mythological images of Christmas. You know the kind. Here's the Virgin Mary, looking perfectly coiffed and with her makeup intact after giving birth. Here's a blue-eyed baby Jesus who actually glows in the dark.

These days, though, the trend is toward generic holiday greetings with family photos. By far my favorite this past year was the one sent to us by a young family with a four-year-old daughter. The design of the card lacked a built-in Christmas message, so the family included one of their own: their little girl's spontaneous explanation of the reason for the season. "Christmas," she said, "is about Jesus and loving other people. Like if they fall down, you don't laugh at them, you help them get back up."

Four years old, and she already understands compassion. There may be hope for us yet.

In this chapter, our task is to explore the themes of compassion and sabbath rest.[1] To this point I've referred to these two qualities, as well as hope and humility, as clinical virtues. More properly, though less conveniently, we might say that hope, humility, and compassion are the actual virtues, while sabbath rest is a spiritual practice that supports them. Today we will first return to the theme of poverty of spirit as an entry point into a consideration of compassion in the life, ministry, and teaching of Jesus. We will look at compassion as a clinical virtue, as well as its flip side, *compassion fatigue*. The problems of burnout and compassion fatigue have led many writers to preach the need for therapist self-care. Christian therapists, however, can benefit from something more, and I will suggest sabbath rest as a theological complement to the recommendations regarding self-care in the clinical literature. My argument will be that we need to regularly take advantage of some form of sabbath-like practice to maintain the narrative coherence and integrity of our vocation.

In the previous chapter, I suggested that therapists who understand themselves as peacemakers might imagine those who seek their services as being poor in spirit. We might add that this is not simply a matter of their clients' emotional state, but of their social position, of the stigma, shame, and interpersonal rejection that is often associated with needing this kind of help in the first place. Psychologist Stephen Hinshaw, in a recent memoir of growing up in the shadow of his father's bipolar disorder, referred to stigma as "another kind of madness."[2] His parents had felt the constant pressure to keep the father's illness a secret lest his career as a professor be jeopardized. Their doctor even encouraged them to keep it from the children, leaving the kids to wonder where Dad had disappeared to during his long hospitalizations. It wasn't until Hinshaw was leaving for college that the truth came out, little

---

1. Practice varies as to whether the word "sabbath" should be capitalized. I have elected to capitalize it only when referring directly to the day or observance itself as "the Sabbath."

2. Hinshaw, *Another Kind of Madness*.

by little, helping him at last to make sense of the puzzles of his childhood.

Unfortunately, the problem of mental health stigma remains persistent and widespread. Bernice Pescosolido, for example, has examined nationally representative data on attitudes in the United States toward mental illness across five decades. In the 1950s, when people were asked to describe "mental illness," they would typically list symptoms that would be associated only with extreme psychosis. Efforts to educate the public since then have helped; Americans now have a broader understanding of mental illness, and are more likely to embrace neurobiological explanations. Ironically, however, such explanations sometimes backfire. Genetically-based understandings can contribute to the perception that the mentally ill are fundamentally flawed in ways that no treatment can fix. Thus, even if public perceptions have become somewhat more sophisticated, stereotypes and stigma persist across sociodemographic groups. Americans still see the mentally ill as prone to violence and thus to be feared, and the more severe a person's mental health issues are perceived to be, the less willing others are to associate with them. In fact, studies using hypothetical vignettes have shown that it is not merely a person's behavior that elicits social rejection; the very label of "mental illness" itself appears to prompt the desire to distance oneself from the person in question.[3]

Unfortunately, there is also evidence that similar confusion and stigmatization exist within the church. One study, for example, used online discussion groups to recruit eighty-five participants who identified themselves both as Christians and as mentally ill. The majority of the sample suffered from anxiety and mood disorders, and over three quarters of the participants were currently in treatment. Participants were required to have sought help from their church at least once; over half had actually sought help several times. They were hoping to get guidance and support, but many reported that their churches failed to respond at all, or that

3. Pescosolido, "Public Stigma of Mental Illness."

the responses they received made the situation worse. Unhelpful responses included being told that:

- they didn't really have a mental illness, even though they had a formal diagnosis (reported by 41.2 percent of the sample);
- they should stop taking their medication (28.2 percent);
- their illness was the result of personal sin (36.5 percent);
- their illness was the result of demonic activity (34.1 percent).[4]

Not everyone who studies church attitudes toward mental illness, thankfully, finds such overtly rejecting behavior. But even then, a more general kind of stigma may persist, in which people still perceive the mentally ill as inherently dangerous.[5]

Sensationalist media portrayals of troubled individuals who have resorted to violence are part of the problem, and further public education may help. Even those of us who supposedly know better, however, may need to monitor our own behavior and speech more carefully. On any given Sunday morning we may worry together over the latest reports of seemingly random acts of violence, and it is right that we should be concerned and pray for peace. But as I suggested in the first chapter, we need to be aware of the unintended consequences of how we talk about such events or about mental illness in general. For example, I must confess with some embarrassment my own unthinking lack of sensitivity in that regard. Not long ago, during a Bible lesson, I made an offhand joke about hearing voices, and people chuckled. Then I remembered that there were people in the room whom I knew had been hospitalized for just that symptom. *Mea culpa*: I am guilty of going for the easy laugh without thinking about the inappropriateness of it or who might be hurt. Fortunately, I know that these individuals are gracious enough to cut me some slack. But that does not in any way excuse my shortsightedness.

4. Stanford and McAlister, "Perceptions of Serious Mental Illness."

5. E.g., Gray, "Attitude of the Public to Mental Health." Gray's study was of an Anglican congregation in the UK.

EMBODYING THE COMPASSION AND
HOSPITALITY OF GOD

In the moral calculus of the kingdom of God, the poor in spirit are deserving of our compassion, and Jesus' own teaching and healing ministry illustrate this. Consider, for example, two contrasting stories of healing from the Gospel of John. When Jesus and his disciples came across a beggar who had been born blind, the disciples treated him as a theological curiosity: "Rabbi, who sinned, this man or his parents, that he was born blind?" (John 9:2). The man was blind, not deaf; did they ask their question aloud? If so, the question betrays their own brand of blindness: the inability to see the sufferer as a human being. Jesus took the opportunity to demonstrate the power of God and what it meant for him to be "the light of the world" (v. 5). He healed the man, who later stood up courageously to being interrogated by the Pharisees and became a disciple of Jesus.

Contrast this with the earlier miracle in which Jesus healed a man who had been lame for nearly forty years (John 5:2–15). The healing occurred not far from the temple. When the Jewish leaders noticed him, they didn't think of him as a man who had been miraculously healed by the power of God, but as a law-breaker who was carrying his mat on the Sabbath. They demanded to know who had told him to do this, but the man had no answer, for Jesus had done the deed and then vanished into the crowd. Later, Jesus found the man in the temple, reminded him of the healing, and told him to stop sinning. The response, as John describes it, was that the man "went away and told the Jews that it was Jesus who had made him well" (5:15), resulting directly in the persecution of the one who had graciously healed him.

It is interesting to note that in neither case are we told that the recipient of the miracle had actually asked to be healed. Both were healed anyway, and both unexpectedly found themselves embroiled in controversy. But their responses to Jesus were remarkably different. The blind beggar responded with gratitude and worship; the lame man seems to have bowed to social pressure, betraying the man who made him well by running to the authorities. The point is that Jesus' actions were contingent neither on receiving an appropriate request nor a properly grateful response. Healing, rather, was a tangible display of the compassion of God.

If it is possible to have favorite Greek words, one of mine would be *splagchnizomai*, a verb that suggests having a reaction in one's "bowels" or "innards"—or in colloquial English, "guts." The word is used several times in the Synoptic Gospels, and each time it either describes Jesus or is used by him to point to the compassion of God or of those who would be obedient to God. In Mark 1:41, for example, the word refers to Jesus' compassion for the leper who came to him to be cleansed; in Matthew 20:34, it refers to his compassion for two blind men who cried out for mercy.

One of the most poignant descriptions occurs in Mark 6, where the disciples were so busy with ministry, so pressed by the demands of the crowds, that they didn't even have time to eat. Jesus decided to take them away to a quiet place where they could rest. But when the boat landed, they were again confronted by the crowds who had run ahead on foot. Mark describes Jesus' response: "he had compassion for them, because they were like sheep without a shepherd" (6:34). Descriptions like these have messianic force: God's Messiah must necessarily be a man who has compassion for the downtrodden.

The point is reinforced by Jesus' teaching. In his parables, the word *splagchnizomai* points to the compassion of God, as in the unexpected response of the father who joyfully embraces the returning prodigal who had shamed the family with his behavior (Luke 15:20), or of the king who forgives his servant an unimaginable debt of ten thousand talents (Matt 18:27). The word also describes the compassion of the Samaritan for the man who had been robbed, beaten, and left for dead by the side of the road (Luke 10:33).

Moreover, in the latter two parables, compassion is directly associated with mercy. In Matthew, when the king upbraids the servant for refusing to forgive the comparatively tiny debt owed to him by a fellow slave, he demands, "Should you not have had mercy on your fellow slave, as I had mercy on you?" (Matt 18:33). In Luke, when Jesus asks the lawyer to tell him who had been a neighbor to the robbery victim, the lawyer is forced to respond, "The one who showed him mercy" (Luke 10:37). And don't forget the two blind men in Matthew: they cried out for mercy (20:30–31) and received compassionate healing (v. 34).

All of this is background to why, when I hear Jesus proclaim that the merciful are blessed, I hear in those words the embodiment of the virtue of compassion. At the opening of the Beatitudes, the poor in spirit, those who mourn, and those who are meek are all honored, not because of the intrinsic goodness of their state of being, but because of the goodness and mercy of God. Jesus then says, "Blessed are those who hunger and thirst for righteousness, for they will be filled" (Matt 5:6). The words "hunger and thirst" echo the theme of poverty and powerlessness, but with a twist: what they desire is *righteousness*. A better way to say this might be that those who understand God's mercy to the weak hunger for *justice*—they long to see God make things right. And it is at this point that the Beatitudes then take an outward turn: "Blessed are the merciful, for they will receive mercy" (Matt 5:7). Those who truly hunger for justice and shalom, in other words, are those who strive to embody the righteous mercy and compassion of God themselves. In return, they receive an eschatological promise: one day, what they long to see done *will* be done, just as Jesus taught them to pray (Matt 6:10).

Most therapists, I would assume, are motivated to some degree by a compassion characterized by what psychologist Kristin Neff has called the "recognition and clear seeing of suffering" coupled with an empathic desire to help.[6] For Christian therapists who view themselves as peacemakers, however, the virtue of compassion would ideally take on additional meaning. They would see the psychological poverty of their clients and respond with other-oriented humility and compassion. The continued cultivation of

---

6. Neff, *Self-Compassion*, 10. Neff also includes what she calls a sense of *common humanity*, i.e., the knowledge that suffering is part of our "shared human condition" (10).

compassion, conversely, would help them stay attuned to the need in the first place. And in eschatological hope, they would envision their clinical work as taken up into God's ongoing ministry of mercy and take heart at every sign of shalom they are privileged to witness, however small it might seem.

Drawing even further upon Christian tradition, therapists might think of compassion as being expressed in the hospitality they show to their clients by providing safe, welcoming spaces.[7] Early Christians were known for their hospitality to traveling strangers.[8] They drew upon the example of Abraham, who offered extravagant hospitality to three visiting strangers without realizing that he was entertaining the Lord himself (Gen 18:1–15). They remembered that Moses spoke of a God who "executes justice for the orphan and the widow, and who loves the strangers, providing them food and clothing" (Deut 10:18), and then commanded God's people to "love the stranger, for you were strangers in the land of Egypt" (v. 19). And, of course, they remembered the teaching of Jesus, who declared:

> When the Son of Man comes in his glory, and all the angels with him, then he will sit on the throne of his glory. All the nations will be gathered before him, and he will separate people one from another as a shepherd separates the sheep from the goats, and he will put the sheep at his right hand and the goats at the left. Then the king will say to those at his right hand, "Come, you that are blessed by my Father, inherit the kingdom prepared for you from the foundation of the world; for I was hungry and you gave me food, I was thirsty and you gave me something to drink, I was a stranger and you welcomed me, I was naked and you gave me clothing, I was sick and you took care of me, I was in prison and you visited me." Then the righteous will answer him, "Lord, when was it that we saw you hungry and gave you food, or thirsty and gave you something to drink? And when was it that we

7. I am indebted to my friend and former colleague Jim Furrow for this insight.

8. E.g., Winner, *Mudhouse Sabbath*, 40–53.

saw you a stranger and welcomed you, or naked and gave
you clothing? And when was it that we saw you sick or in
prison and visited you?" And the king will answer them,
"Truly I tell you, just as you did it to one of the least of
these who are members of my family, you did it to me."
(Matt 25:31–40)

Over the centuries, Christians have written in different ways about
how Jesus might actually be present in the stranger.[9] Whatever
the truth of the matter, the point is that those who are blessed by
the king are those who welcomed strangers, who offered compassion and hospitality to "the least of these" without knowing that
they were ministering by proxy to the king himself. They did it
because it was the right thing to do, not because they expected to
be rewarded.

What might a clinical embodiment of hospitality look like?
One suggestion is to consider how clients might experience the
physical space in which therapy occurs: is it warm and welcoming,
or filled with symbols of the therapist's power? But hospitality is
also about the quality of the therapeutic relationship itself. Referring to the ordinary act of having guests, Lauren Winner worries
that our pride may keep us from inviting others over unless the
house is spotless. She writes:

My mother set a high standard. Her house is always immaculate, most especially if she's expecting company. But
if I wait for immaculate, I will never have a guest. . . . We
are not meant simply to invite people into our homes, but
also to invite them into our lives. . . . [W]e are not meant
to rearrange our lives for our guests—we are meant to
invite our guests to enter into our lives as they are.[10]

That doesn't just mean letting others see our messy living rooms,
but something of our messy lives, our personal faults and flaws.

9. E.g., Oden, *And You Welcomed Me*, an annotated collection of ancient
Christian writing on the theme of hospitality; the passage from Matthew 25 is
cited frequently.

10. Winner, *Mudhouse Sabbath*, 50.

Her words make me wonder: can therapists envision judicious uses of self-disclosure as acts of hospitality?

And what might change if they did?

THE COST OF COMPASSION

None of this is meant to suggest that it is a simple matter to maintain a consistently compassionate or hospitable stance. Those who study stress and trauma refer frequently to the experience of *compassion fatigue*.[11] As Charles Figley explains:

> The very act of being compassionate and empathic extracts a cost under most circumstances. In our effort to view the world from the perspective of the suffering we suffer. The meaning of compassion is to bear suffering. Compassion fatigue, like any other kind of fatigue, reduces our capacity or our interest in bearing the suffering of others.[12]

As we have noted before, the life of the psychotherapist or mental health professional is not an easy one. The same can be said of other helping professionals, including nurses, social workers, trauma specialists, even pastors. There is an emotional, physical, and social price to be paid when people set themselves to enter deeply into the pain and suffering of others on a regular basis.

For therapists, part of the difficulty has to do with the simple fact that some clients are easier to work with and more likeable, while others can strain the patience of even the most seasoned practitioner. Jeff Kottler, for example, has painted a somewhat tongue-in-cheek composite portrait of what many therapists might consider to be the "ideal client":

> They are bright, vibrant, and interesting people. They are professionals. They are reasonably healthy, have no underlying personality disorder, and present

11. The term was reputedly introduced in the nursing literature in 1992 by Joinson, "Coping with Compassion Fatigue."

12. Figley, "Compassion Fatigue," 1434.

symptomatology that is easy to treat. They are highly motivated to change, yet are patient enough to wait for results. They have a great capacity for developing insight, can tolerate ambiguity, and have a high threshold for dealing with uncertainty. They are verbally expressive, creative thinkers who present vivid material rich in detail and symbolism. They are socially skilled and responsible. They show up on time, pay their bills promptly, and offer to pay for cancellations. They would never call therapists at home or bother us between sessions unless they had a genuine emergency. They are appropriately deferential toward and respectful of our position. They are also very grateful for our help.[13]

What therapist wouldn't wish to have more clients like that? Ironically, though, one wonders why such a person would need a therapist in the first place. Wouldn't a good self-help book do?

The reality, of course, is that clients and caseloads are a good deal more trying and complex. Ostensibly, clients come seeking help, but their persistent behavior both during and between sessions leaves their therapists wondering if they really want to change—or are even capable of it. Some clients, in fact, seem bent on defeating their therapists, actively or passively, as if needing to demonstrate that therapy is a hopeless cause. In response, therapists run the gamut of emotions working with them, from exasperation to boredom, struggling with doubts about their own competence, feeling their compassion stretched to the limit.

But even with the most cooperative and grateful of clients, there is still a personal price to be paid when one is expected to continually empathize with suffering—particularly when working with trauma survivors. At the extremes, in a phenomenon known as *vicarious traumatization*, therapists and other helpers can themselves become traumatized by the exposure.[14] In less severe cases, helpers may still experience *secondary traumatic stress*; working empathetically with traumatic material puts a strain on the helper's

13. Kottler, *Compassionate Therapy*, 31–32.

14. The language of *vicarious traumatization* was introduced by McCann and Pearlman in 1990 in "Vicarious Traumatization."

emotional state and ability to cope, and may lead to symptoms similar to Post-Traumatic Stress Disorder.[15]

And even when therapists are not working directly or extensively with trauma, they must still deal with the significant personal demands that are intrinsic to their vocation. One source reports that as many as 60 percent of psychotherapists will experience a psychiatric disorder at some point in their lives; 25 percent will experience suicidal ideation; over 6 percent will actually make a suicide attempt.[16] Therapists and other helping professionals are subject to *burnout*, a negative emotional state which can arise in virtually any work setting in which people have too much work to do with too few resources, and little in the way of a sense of control over one's situation.

In its classic formulation by Christina Maslach, burnout is characterized by "emotional exhaustion, depersonalization, and reduced sense of personal accomplishment."[17] In other words, helpers who are burned out feel depleted and empty, begin to develop negative attitudes toward those whom they are supposed to serve, and finally begin to feel negatively about themselves. One therapist who worked with survivors of childhood sexual abuse described her burnout in these terms: "I think I get overwhelmed, and overwhelmed for me comes in two forms: I get physically, emotionally and mentally exhausted, and I also become emotionally shutdown and I am not as emotionally responsive to people. I feel like I don't have any more to give, it is all used up and gone."[18] Other therapists in the same study spoke of forgetting things that needed to be done, being plagued by intrusive thoughts, losing sleep, and becoming less patient and more agitated with others. We can think of compassion fatigue as the unfortunate combination of

---

15. The language of *secondary traumatic stress* is emphasized by Stamm; e.g., Stamm, *Secondary Traumatic Stress*. In a slightly different manner, Figley defines compassion fatigue as a secondary traumatic stress response which is "nearly identical to PTSD"; Figley, "Compassion Fatigue," 1435.

16. Teater and Ludgate, *Overcoming Compassion Fatigue*, chap. 1, table 3.

17. Maslach, *Burnout*, 2.

18. Killian, "Helping Till it Hurts?," 35.

both burnout *and* secondary traumatic stress—a perfect storm of work characteristics that drains therapists of their ability to sustain compassion.[19]

Relatively speaking, research on compassion fatigue is still in its early stages. A recently published review article, however, examined thirty-two studies on compassion fatigue in mental health professionals.[20] Three main risk factors and one potential protective factor were identified. The first and most important risk factor was the professional's own *trauma history*: those who had experienced their own traumatic life events were more likely to experience compassion fatigue. The second factor, *empathy*, moderated this relationship; those who were more empathetic to begin with were more likely to experience compassionate fatigue as a result of how their clients' trauma stirred up unresolved issues related to their own trauma history. A third factor, *caseload*, makes straightforward sense: the more time professionals spent working with trauma, or the higher the proportion of trauma clients in their caseload, the greater the risk of secondary traumatic stress and compassion fatigue.[21] Fourth and finally, the authors noted the potentially protective factor of *mindfulness*. More mindful professionals, i.e. those with the ability to be non-judgmentally aware of their own cognitions and mental states, had lower compassion fatigue scores. It is with such findings in mind that writers in the field emphasize how crucial self-care is to the well-being of therapists and by extension, the well-being of those whom they serve.

Before moving into a discussion of self-care and sabbath, however, I want to take a moment to circle back to the clinical virtues of hope and humility. Again, our clients have been humbled by life and come seeking hope, which they find in part through

19. This conceptualization follows Beth Hudnall Stamm's construct of *professional quality of life*, of which compassion fatigue is one part. Stamm's Professional Quality of Life Scale (ProQOL) is one of the most widely used measures in the research on compassion fatigue. Stamm, *Concise ProQOL Manual*.

20. Turgoose and Maddox, "Predictors of Compassion Fatigue."

21. E.g., Baird and Kracen, "Vicarious Traumatization and Secondary Traumatic Stress."

our compassionate care. This may be particularly true of those who have lived through trauma. But the research on burnout and compassion fatigue suggests that compassion—perhaps the most intuitively obvious of the clinical virtues—needs to be sustained by our own hope and humility. It's not just a matter of approaching clinical work humbly, but how we respond when the work itself humbles us.

Cultivating the clinical virtues entails changing the way we think, and engaging our eschatological imagination. People who work with compassion fatigue from a cognitive-behavioral point of view, for example, note that one of the risk factors is the therapist's potentially unrealistic or irrational cognitions. These may include beliefs about their clients, such as the following:

- My clients should not be difficult, resistant or challenging;

- They should work as hard as I do to make treatment work;

- All my client sessions should be as the textbooks describe;

- I should never be disrespected or criticized by a client;

- Clients should be motivated to change and to fully engage in treatment;

- I should be loved and admired by my clients.[22]

Similarly, therapists may hold unhelpful beliefs about themselves and their work, including one or more of the following:

- I must be successful with all my clients;

- If I am not successful in alleviating clients' problems, I can't feel good about myself;

- I should not dislike any of my clients;

- I should have all the answers;

- I should not have any emotional reactions myself and, if I do, I should control them and never show this to clients or colleagues;

22. Teater and Ludgate, *Overcoming Compassion Fatigue*, loc. 1095.

- My worth as a person is dependent on my job performance;
- I will be seen as weak if I ask for help;
- Other people should see things my way;
- I must be perceived as totally competent.[23]

This is not to say, of course, that we are consciously aware of holding such beliefs. If I were to ask you directly if you believe that clients will never disrespect you, or that you should have all the answers, you would probably tell me, "No, of course not." But the real question is how you respond when a client does in fact disrespect you—sometimes rather egregiously!—or when you find that you don't have the answer you think you should have and feel lost.

The vocation of entering into the suffering of others with sustained compassion places a heavy personal demand on therapists, and those who hold the kind of beliefs just mentioned are less likely to engage in appropriate self-care or get the help they need. Just as it is with our clients, it takes humility to acknowledge when we need help. And for Christians, it takes hope to keep humility in its proper eschatological context. In Henri Nouwen's memorable phrase, therapists are "wounded healers," ministering out of their own suffering to the suffering of others.[24] What gives us hope is the knowledge that God not only champions those who live in poverty of spirit, mourning, and meekness, but calls them to participate in the work of making peace through the ministry of compassion. We can be humbled by the work we do and by our seeming failures without having to believe that this somehow disqualifies us from the vocation. And again, even in the most difficult of sessions, we can draw encouragement from each moment of shalom as a sign of our participation in the peacemaking work of God.

23. Teater and Ludgate, *Overcoming Compassion Fatigue*, loc. 1105.
24. Nouwen, *Wounded Healer*.

REST FOR THE WEARY

Thus we turn to a discussion of self-care and its relationship to sabbath practice. Figley reminds us that self-care "need not be enigmatic, expansive, or expensive. In fact, it is often the simplest of strategies that makes the greatest difference."[25] Some strategies are already implied by the previous discussion and echoed in the self-care literature: recognize the risks and demands associated being a therapist; watch out for unrealistic cognitions; seek therapy as needed; diversify your caseload.[26] Neff would add that we need to learn *self-compassion* as well, by being mindful of our distress, treating ourselves with kindness instead of criticism, and recognizing that suffering and failure are part of our shared human condition.[27] Indeed, as the authors of one recent study found, therapists who were higher in self-compassion were less likely to experience burnout or compassion fatigue.[28]

Some trauma therapists who were asked about their self-care strategies emphasized the need to debrief with other people and engage in activities that help alleviate or manage stress, such as socializing with friends and spending time with family, or finding enjoyable ways to get exercise. They also mentioned the importance of spirituality, of being guided and sustained by something larger than themselves.[29] Similar recommendations are found in an article written for marital and family therapists:

> Engaging in light-hearted conversation, watching comedy entertainment, practicing religion, and participating in noncompetitive activities or hobbies may also reduce stress and increase happiness. The overall idea is to avoid

---

25. Figley and Ludick, "Secondary Traumatization and Compassion Fatigue," 582.

26. See, e.g., recommendations #1, 7, 8, and 9 in Norcross, "Psychotherapist Self-Care."

27. Neff, *Self-Compassion*.

28. Beaumont et al., "Measuring Relationships."

29. Killian, "Helping Till it Hurts?"

stress, increase relaxation, and be part of a world that
does not mirror that of the therapeutic setting.[30]

I affirm the practical suggestions contained in those two sentences.
At the same time, however, I'm concerned about the implications
of listing religion as a self-care strategy, all in the same breath with
watching funny movies and having hobbies. *Be religious,* we're
told, *because it's good for you.* Surely there's some truth to that. But
it's only a partial truth, and one that leaves distortions of our sense
of identity or vocation untouched. If sabbath practice becomes
nothing more than an escape from the stress of our jobs, it may fail
at helping us cultivate a right sense of our vocation.

In both Exodus and Deuteronomy, the injunction to remember the Sabbath and keep it holy (Exod 20:8; Deut 5:12) is
the fourth and longest of the Ten Commandments. In Exodus,
the rationale for the observance is that God rested on the seventh
day and therefore consecrated it (Exod 20:11). In Deuteronomy,
the people are reminded that God rescued them out of slavery in
Egypt, and thus the Sabbath is to be a holy day of rest for all of
God's people, their children, their slaves, their animals—and even
any resident aliens in their midst (Deut 5:14–15).

But many American Christians, I think, have an ambivalent
relationship to the very notion of commandment. We cherish our
freedom, and freedom often means not having to do anything
we don't want to do unless it's truly necessary. We honor the Ten
Commandments in principle, but in practice, the fourth commandment is either treated as one of the unnecessary ones or
transmuted into a strongly worded recommendation that we get
ourselves to church on Sunday.

Unfortunately, the very idea of a sabbath commandment may
trigger a negative and defensive reaction in those who grew up
with legalistic traditions of sabbath observance. I have no interest
in trying to pressure anyone to adopt some new set of rules that
have no personal resonance. But I do want to suggest the possibility of receiving sabbath as a *gift.*

30. Negash and Sahin, "Compassion Fatigue in Marriage and Family
Therapy," 9–10.

Think, for example, of the story of manna in the wilderness. God provided food for his people because they needed it to survive. Every day, they were to go out and gather as much as they needed for their families, not keeping any until the next day or it would spoil. No manna was given on the seventh day, because it was the day of rest—so the people were commanded to gather a double portion on the sixth day, with the promise that it would not spoil. Still, some of the people went out to do the work of gathering on the seventh day, prompting God to say to Moses, "How long will you refuse to keep my commandments and instructions? See! The LORD has given you the sabbath, therefore on the sixth day he gives you food for two days" (Exod 16:28–29).[31] Here, there is both commandment and gift: the Lord gives food and the Lord gives sabbath rest, providing for both the physical and spiritual well-being of his people. Commandment and gift are not incompatible when the covenant love of God is their source.

Or consider the words of Jesus: "The sabbath was made for humankind, and not humankind for the sabbath; so the Son of Man is lord even of the sabbath" (Mark 2:27–28). This is the response Jesus gave to the Pharisees who were criticizing his hungry disciples for picking grain in violation of the Sabbath. I suspect that some of us, unconsciously steeped in individualistic values, might hear Jesus as telling the Pharisees, "Don't quote rules to me. I have more authority than you. These guys are with me, and I say it's okay." We're satisfied that Jesus has won yet another argument with those hidebound hypocrites. Freedom has triumphed again over legalism, and we can move on with the story. But again, have we missed the possibility of receiving a gift? *The Sabbath was made for humankind*, in a way that assures our hunger will be fed.

Still, sabbath rest can be a hard sell. I once spoke on the subject of rest at another seminary, to a group of students and local pastors. There seemed to be a bit of a generational divide in response to the lecture. The younger members of the audience seemed to resonate with the idea of rest, while a few of the older members looked agitated. At the end of the presentation, one of

31. The NRSV does not capitalize "sabbath."

87

the pastors stood and angrily asked a question that sounded more like an accusation: "Do you mean to tell me that I'm supposed to ask the members of my congregation to give me a day off when they're working so hard in the church themselves?"

The question grieved me, but not because I was personally offended by it. With sadness, I imagined a congregation of people scurrying about doing what everyone took for granted as the Lord's work, subtly (or not so subtly!) competing with one another to see who could win more honor through their sacrifices of time or effort. In such a congregational culture, rest is neither a commandment nor a gift: it's a sign of spiritual laziness, of shirking responsibility, of shameful selfishness. To use another of Brueggemann's metaphors, we sometimes act as if we were still slaves in Egypt, commanded to make bricks without straw.[32] We can give neither ourselves nor each other *permission* to rest, whatever the commandment might say.

The pressures of work are both external and internal. There are things to be done and obligations to fulfill that vary with our stage and station in life. Leisure time and the freedom to be able to decide what we do with our days can be marks of economic privilege; some people literally can't afford to take a day off. And even when we have such freedom, we can put pressure on ourselves, feeling like we don't deserve to rest until all of our work is done.

But the reality for responsible people is that our work is never done. As Jewish scholar Abraham Heschel once wrote regarding the Sabbath, "Is it *possible* for a human being to do all of his [or her] work in six days? Does not our work always remain incomplete?"[33] In other words, if we wait for our work to be done before we believe we've earned our rest, we'll never rest, to the detriment of body and soul. Dorothy Bass quotes the wonderfully wise words of a teacher who was musing with her colleagues about work and rest. Conscientious teachers, as we know, are never done with work: there is always more lesson planning to do, or grading, or a hundred other

32. Brueggemann, *Sabbath as Resistance*.

33. Heschel, *Sabbath*, 32, emphasis added. The quotation has been slightly reworded to reflect inclusive language.

tasks that take up their evenings and weekends. But this teacher decided she needed to take a stand. "Show me a person who can't get their work done in six days," she declared, "and I'll show you a person who can't get their work done in seven."[34]

Sabbath rest is not simply the religious equivalent of a day off from work. The very notion of a "day off" is a negative one, suggesting the need to escape our brickmaking for the sake of our sanity. If we have the means, we "vacate" or "get away"—and then return to the same job, perhaps slightly better rested physically but with the same attitude. This is not sabbath rest. We may enjoy leisure activities on the Sabbath, but sabbath rest is not to be identified with leisure. It is not simply an opportunity to get away from work, to do things to recharge our batteries, but to cultivate a right relationship to our work. Again, to quote Heschel:

> To the biblical mind . . . the Sabbath as a day of rest, as a day of abstaining from toil, is not for the purpose of recovering one's lost strength and becoming fit for the forthcoming labor. The Sabbath is a day for the sake of life. [Human beings are not beasts] of burden, and the Sabbath is not for the purpose of enhancing the efficiency of [their] work.[35]

It's an opportunity to remember who we are: the beloved children of a God who blesses the poor in spirit, who feeds those who wander in the desert. We need to be secure in that identity in order to be rightly related to our work. Toward that end, Heschel insists, the Sabbath "is a day in which we abandon our plebeian pursuits and reclaim our authentic state, in which we may partake of a blessedness in which we are what we are, regardless of whether we are learned or not, of whether our career is a success or a failure; it is a day of independence of social conditions."[36]

To be clear, I am not suggesting that Christian therapists ignore the advice offered in the literature on self-care, burnout,

34. Bass, *Receiving the Day*, 60.

35. Heschel, *Sabbath*, 14. The quotation has been reworded to reflect inclusive language.

36. Heschel, *Sabbath*, 30.

and compassion fatigue. I am not denigrating the value of play, relaxation, or diversion. But as Christians, we need more than just escape or distraction, more than a day of vacation or binge-watching on Netflix. Sabbath rest is not simply about forgetting work but about remembering who God is—and who we are as a consequence. We need a regular discipline that will help us remember that our worth is not defined by our work, that our value is not measured by our productivity.

This, I fear, is an occupational hazard for working professionals. I was thinking about this recently while teaching my way through the Gospel of John on Sunday mornings. Jesus has washed his disciples' feet, including those of Judas the betrayer, who has run off into the night. Jesus is bidding the remainder of the Twelve farewell, trying to prepare them for his departure and what they will have to endure after he's gone. He promises to not leave them as orphans; he promises to send them the Holy Spirit. And then he proclaims that last of the great "I Am" sayings in John's Gospel:

> I am the true vine, and my Father is the vinegrower. He removes every branch in me that bears no fruit. Every branch that bears fruit he prunes to make it bear more fruit. You have already been cleansed by the word that I have spoken to you. Abide in me as I abide in you. Just as the branch cannot bear fruit by itself unless it abides in the vine, neither can you unless you abide in me. I am the vine, you are the branches. Those who abide in me and I in them bear much fruit, because apart from me you can do nothing. Whoever does not abide in me is thrown away like a branch and withers; such branches are gathered, thrown into the fire, and burned. If you abide in me, and my words abide in you, ask for whatever you wish, and it will be done for you. My Father is glorified by this, that you bear much fruit and become my disciples. As the Father has loved me, so I have loved you; abide in my love. If you keep my commandments, you will abide in my love, just as I have kept my Father's commandments and abide in his love. I have said these things to you so that my joy may be in you, and that your joy may be complete. (John 15:1–11)

The metaphor of the vine isn't something Jesus made up on the spot; he is drawing upon Old Testament imagery of Israel as a vine planted and tended by God to bear fruit. Through their disobedience, however, Israel produced only "wild grapes," prompting God to withdraw his care and protection (Isa 5:4–5; cf. also Ps 80:8–16). Jesus is the "true" vine because he is the embodiment of all that the people of God were meant to be. Thus, there is a legitimate element of warning to what Jesus says; some branches may be cut away and thrown onto the fire for their lack of proper fruit. Perhaps that's why that pastor was so upset with me for suggesting that people in ministry need to honor the commandment to rest. Aren't we always supposed to be about the business of producing fruit? Who wants to be chopped off and burned?

I believe that such an anxious reading of Jesus' words, however, misrepresents what he is saying. Jesus is, after all, trying to comfort his disciples, not threaten them. He's promising a continuing relationship with them, a relationship of love and joy. And though it is true that Jesus wants them to bear fruit, he does not actually command them to do so. He commands them instead to *abide* in him and in his love, even as he promises to abide in them. They are branches, and their very life draws upon the vine. He's not saying, "If you don't bear fruit, you'll be thrown on the fire." He's saying, "If you don't abide, you will wither, and then what use will you be?" That's not a threat, but a warning, on the order of telling someone, "If you don't eat, you will die."

So much of my professional life and consciousness is about productivity. As a teacher, I'm always working on the next lecture, Bible lesson, or speaking engagement. As a minister, it's the next sermon or wedding or memorial service. As a writer, it's the next article or book or blog post. I'm not a list-maker by nature, but I'm forced to make lists just to keep track of my responsibilities and commitments, and some part of my brain is always thinking about the next thing on the list. I wake up at night and start thinking about the projects I'm working on, crafting sentences in my head, trying to hang onto ideas that I want to remember in the morning, unable to go back to sleep because I can't turn off my brain.

I understand the need to be fruitful. As Jesus said, the Father is glorified when we bear much fruit. But to be completely honest, I'm not sure about my motivation: how much do I pursue fruitfulness for the sake of my own glory instead of the Father's? To what extent do I feel the need to be productive to have a sense of personal worth? That's the convenient thing about being Christian professionals: we can take on project after project for egoistic reasons and convince ourselves that it's all for God. How can we know the difference? Here's a litmus test: how good are we at abiding? Personally, I'm good at finding new things to put on lists. But I'm much less adept at abiding.

Am I the only one?

Moreover, the fruit of which Jesus speaks is not to be identified with the tasks and accomplishments we put on our to-do lists and vitae. At best, these are but vehicles for fruitfulness and not the fruit themselves. The older I get, the more I am reminded of Paul's image of a coming day in which the quality of our work will be tested by fire (1 Cor 3:10–15). Will anything I have done survive the test? The measure will not be sales figures, impact ratings, or number of views, "likes," or "follows" online. The measure will be the growth and spread of the kind of fruit God cares about, like love, joy, and of course, peace (Gal 5:22).

If we are to enjoy the gift of sabbath, we will need to move in two directions. Shalom, as we have seen, has both negative and positive aspects, absence and presence. Similarly, the enjoyment of sabbath rest entails both "Thou shalt not" and "Thou shalt."[37] Thou shalt not, of course, *work*—which sounds simple enough as a concept but can be difficult to put into practice. Rabbinic teaching identified dozens of kinds of activities that were thought to constitute work, creating a complex web of rules and regulations which many of the Jewish people themselves failed to heed.[38] How does one know what is and what isn't work? If you're in paid Christian ministry and regularly read and study Scripture and theology, is

---

37. As observed by Winner, *Mudhouse Sabbath*, 4–5.

38. I think here particularly of Chaim Grade's touching memoir *My Mother's Sabbath Days*.

that "work" and therefore to be avoided on the Sabbath? Such are the puzzles we confront when we make sabbath more a matter of behavior than of the spirit. To be sure, therapists who teach time and stress management to their clients know that we must commit to some behavioral boundaries or nothing will change. We must firmly and consistently say no to some things in order to say yes to others.

But sabbath rest is not guaranteed by having a don't-do list. Our work activities are not the problem in themselves; the issue is our relationship to our work. To what extent have we effectively begun to worship productivity or some other form of success, to give it the allegiance that belongs only to God? Or to what extent have the rhythms and assumptions of the work week come to define how we approach life overall? Sabbath is consecrated time; but how can we experience the sacredness of time when we're accustomed to perceiving it in terms of the fifty-minute billable hour?

We establish boundaries, therefore, in order to define a space of freedom in which our worth is not defined by what we do. During designated sabbath time, therefore, I try to stay away from activities that feel like personal and professional responsibilities or accomplishments, anything that might belong on a to-do list or contribute another line to my vita. I don't send or answer email. I try to avoid anything that draws me back into what I call "the measured life"—all the different ways in which we daily quantify how well our lives are supposedly going. I don't step on the bathroom scale. I don't wear my fitness tracker. I don't use apps that chart my progress in some way. I stay off social media. Why? Because all of these link my worth in some way to measurable goals. *Blessed are the slim. Blessed are the active. Blessed are those whose feet are firmly planted on the paths of self-improvement. And blessed are you when people like you, and follow you, and post all kinds of happy emojis on your Facebook page. Rejoice and be glad, for in this way you know your life matters.* Do we know the extent to which our daily habits and practices, even those that are supposedly for our own benefit, draw us away from the awareness that we are deeply and truly loved by a God who champions the poor in spirit?

SAYING YES TO RENEWAL

We must say no, then, to make room for yes. But yes to what? Rest, of course; by all means, take that much-needed nap. Indeed, I've found that the more I get accustomed to a regular sabbath rhythm, the more my mind and body seem able to let down and accept their tiredness on a day of rest. As Marva Dawn has suggested, however, sabbath is not just about ceasing and resting, but about what she calls *embracing* and *feasting*. She writes:

> All the great motifs of our Christian faith are under-scored in our Sabbath keeping. Its Ceasing deepens our repentance for the many ways that we fail to trust God and try to create our own future. Its Resting strengthens our faith in the totality of his grace. Its Embracing invites us to take the truths of our faith and apply them practically in our values and lifestyles. Its Feasting heightens our sense of eschatological hope—the Joy of our present experience of God's love and its foretaste of the Joy to come.[39]

A day of rest can be more than just an escape from stress; it is an opportunity to be renewed in hope by abiding in the love of Christ. One could argue, of course, that it is possible to abide in Christ without having to set aside an entire day to do it! And again, it is not my desire to legislate questions of how long and how often when it comes to rest. When Jesus speaks of abiding, however, surely he means something less like discrete behaviors and more like a disposition. If that is so, then it's worth asking ourselves what disciplines we might need to form such a disposition. I submit that sabbath is one such discipline: the deliberate, habitual practice of setting aside a regular time consecrated to God in which we might enjoy rest and renewal.

Here's another way to think of it. Early family therapists made a great deal out of the concept of *homeostasis*, a term coined by physiologist Walter Cannon in the years after World War I. It re-fers to all the ways in which the human body automatically tries to

39. Dawn, *Keeping the Sabbath Wholly*, 203.

maintain itself in a state of constancy and equilibrium. In the dead of winter or the height of summer, for example, our bodies work to maintain a core temperature that usually varies by no more than a degree or two, while we remain unaware of the processes involved. One physician recently summed up just how revolutionary the idea of homeostasis was at the time:

> Cannon's insight inverted long-established logic. Physiologists, for generations, had described animals as assemblages of machines . . . Muscles were motors; the heart a pump; the nerves electrical conduits. . . . [T]he emphasis was on movement, on actions, on work—*Don't just stand there, do something.* . . . Cannon . . . had fundamentally changed our conception of how the human body works. A major point of physiological "activity," paradoxically, was to enable stasis. *Don't just do something, stand there.*[40]

I wonder if we need our logic inverted as well. Could it be that the God who created humanity knows what we need to maintain our spiritual homeostasis? Do we constantly push ourselves out of equilibrium by the way we work, even by the way we think about work?

Then don't just do something, stand there.

There's no one-size-fits-all formula for sabbath rest. But we might begin by honestly pondering a few questions. What helps us let go of performance anxiety or shame, and to accept once again the compassionate love of God? What helps us to marvel at the grace and majesty of God, and to trust God's wisdom and sovereignty? How might we enjoy the goodness of God's creation, or the company of people in our lives who know our faults and weaknesses but love us anyway? Sabbath can be a time to prayerfully practice whatever helps us to regain our perspective and equilibrium, and to get a firmer hold on our vocation. Again, to quote Marva Dawn: "If we become people of peace through the

---

40. Mukherjee, "Bodies at Rest and in Motion," 30.

intentionality of our Sabbath keeping, then we will, out of that character of peacemaking, live in a way that promotes peace."[41]

To be a psychotherapist is to enter compassionately into the secret suffering of others, over and over and over again, and to carry the burden of holding that suffering in trust. We are privy to the best and the worst of the human spirit, and we can't do such work with any degree of empathy without being affected by it. We need the hope of knowing that the healing ministry into which we have entered belongs first and foremost to God, who has already promised a new heaven and a new earth, a day in which death, sorrow, and pain will be no more (Rev 21:1–4).

The work of renewal has already begun, and we have the privilege of being part of it. Today, that work remains incomplete. We must strive to be the most caring and competent therapists we can be, but even then, we will not be able to help every client. This will humble us and perhaps even feel like failure. But in that humiliation we have the opportunity to learn true humility, the humility of knowing that there is but one Savior—and we aren't it. We have the opportunity of learning to notice and rejoice in every manifestation of shalom in our clients' lives, not as a sign of our clinical brilliance, but as a sign that grace is a living, everpresent reality even in a broken world. We have the opportunity to be renewed in our compassion, particularly if we deliberately set aside sabbath time to abide in the love and mercy of Christ.

We are peacemakers, the children of God who mirror the compassion of God as we play midwife to moments of shalom in the lives of clients. That is our calling, the primary vocation that is embodied in and through our clinical work with those who are downtrodden in spirit. May we embrace that vocation with whole hearts, and integrated imaginations.

41. Dawn, *Keeping the Sabbath Wholly*, 95.

RESPONSE

Miyoung Yoon Hammer

At the heart of the MFT program curriculum is our spiritual formation framework where we focus on the clinical virtues of humility, hope, and compassion and the practice of Sabbath rest. All four virtues, while separate and distinct, hang together with beautiful synergy. Each virtue, when understood alongside the others, has greater complexity. Together they produce a more complete picture of the foundation upon which our students are to begin developing their personal and professional identities as peacemakers in the pursuit of becoming ministers of healing in a suffering world. In this response, I will focus on the virtue of *compassion* and the practice of *Sabbath rest* as I add my own texture and nuance to the ideas about compassion, hospitality, and Sabbath rest that have been described in the previous chapter. My hope is to further affirm the notion that these virtues, along with those described in earlier chapters, are ones that are meant to restore both our communion among ourselves as well as our communion with God.

COMPASSION

As stated in Cameron's chapter on compassion, the "poor in spirit" in the clinical context most often refers to our clients who are in emotional distress, and might also be experiencing rejection, shame, and isolation due to the stigma of therapy and what others think it says about them that they need this type of help. This stigma regarding psychotherapy and the broader field of mental health support services is pervasive and is not defined by boundaries of race, culture, social class, gender, or religion. Although some communities may have a greater familiarity and appreciation for psychotherapy, the stigma persists. I would suggest that more broadly and beyond the therapy room, the poor in spirit includes two groups of people. First, the poor in spirit include those in our society who are marginalized as a result of the misperceptions and assumptions people make about the worth and value of their life based on their level of education, the color of their skin, their sexual identity, their SES, their political or religious affiliations, etc. These who are poor in spirit are cast to the margins in our society, receiving condemnation based on an inherent attribution of their identities, and thus, working their way out of this social location is nearly impossible. The Christian narrative informs our compassionate response to the poor in spirit. As the exemplar of compassion, Jesus ministered to the poor in spirit through his teaching and healing and we are particularly moved by those instances when he healed without the requirement of a request or an expectation of a thanks. The restoration of sight or the ability to walk came unexpectedly to those who were healed.

But there are also stories of Jesus being pursued for his healing powers by individuals who humbly and desperately pleaded for healing. In fact, in some of the stories, it seems that *Jesus* is the one who is surprised. For example, the woman who bled for twelve years and pleaded in desperation by touching Jesus' garment; the story of Jairus who pleaded with Jesus to heal his dying daughter; Mary and Martha who begged that Jesus would heal their brother Lazarus; or the centurion who asked Jesus to heal his servant. Oftentimes the people seeking healing were unlikely suspects, but in asking, in spite of the odds, their faith was revealed. Either out of sheer desperation or irrational conviction, they believed that Jesus could and *would* heal and they were willing to take the risk to ask.

Whenever I hear these stories of healing I construct a scene in my mind where the person approaches Jesus and immediately the crowd comes to a hushed silence. At best, this is awkward. At worst, this is offensive. I'm always struck by these moments and then I consider what must be going on in the heart of the petitioner. When we love someone who is suffering or when we're fighting for life, we are willing to do whatever it takes to find a cure. We gather our courage and find our voice. And then we ask. Like Esther, risking her life for her people as she approached the king without an invitation, we ask. Here, what I'm referring to is the way that compassion is meant to move us beyond empathy and into action. It is important to listen, be present, and sometimes be still and silent alongside those who suffer, much like Job's friends who sat with him in silence for seven days and seven nights. But compassion is kinetic, active, and dynamic and it eventually moves us to action. These two components of compassion, empathy and action, are rooted in the truth that *all* people are God's creation, made in his image and designed for a purpose in his kingdom. Therefore, all who suffer as well as those who cause suffering, are firstly God's creation, entitled to be restored and intended to be made new.

Deep compassion is born out of this belief that the people who stand on either side of suffering and are wrought by pain are in need of shalom, a restored wholeness that allows them to be who God intends for them to be and to live in the freedom of his righteousness and for the fulfillment of his glory. Having compassion means we help them ask by using our God-given gifts to be agents of reconciliation and healing. We recognize that they *are* deserving of our compassion, but we also see that they have a voice to offer and we ought not to rob them of their own voices so that they might ask. We help them learn for the first time, or relearn again, the ability to ask. Our desire is that, like the bleeding woman, they will find their voices to ask for healing even if others around them might not agree that they are deserving of Jesus' compassion.

This isn't a "pull themselves up with their bootstraps" kind of a notion. Not everyone has boots and for some, their boots are so worn that they don't have straps to pull in the first place. But perhaps, having compassion means that we—especially those who have privilege because we belong to the majority group or have power based on our social position or our position as therapists—use our privilege to help the marginalized, the poor in spirit, to put on their boots or to fasten their straps. Perhaps the greatest privilege that we, as Christians, possess is the knowledge of the gospel and the conviction of our faith. From this particular position of privilege, we are compelled to have compassion for the poor in spirit and to share with them the freedom and the courage to ask.

This act of asking is an expression of agency, a construct that is used to describe a person's recognition of and belief in her or his internal resources (i.e., self-worth and value, the possession of a voice, the presence of God) and then using those resources in positive ways for the wellbeing of self and others. Agency is necessary for change because we must believe that we have the ability to affect others or our circumstances and this belief leads us to have hope. Agency bridges the two clinical virtues of compassion and hope. When we see suffering around us, our hearts are pierced and we grieve the wounds and the violence against God's creation. But we aren't meant to remain there. Rather, our hope in God's redemptive power and his promises for a new creation fuels our sense of agency that springs us forth into action and helps actualize growth and transformation.

Most of us first got into this profession because we realized our ability to have extraordinary compassion and empathy for others. Oftentimes I hear from students as they enter our program that they received feedback from others about what good listeners they were and how empathic and compassionate others described them to be; it's almost like a prerequisite for becoming an MFT. But I would suggest that if we limit our understanding of compassion to being our ability to have empathy for our clients and to hold them in their suffering, then we will greatly run the risk of compassion fatigue and burnout. Don't get me wrong, this aspect of compassion is essential to being a good therapist. But our compassion doesn't end there. Our compassion must compel us to *see* our clients and the gifts they possess—see them beyond the diagnosis and the dysfunction. We must continue to see them and help them find their voices so that they will be empowered to *ask*.

HOSPITALITY

Another theme that stood out for me was that of hospitality. This concept of therapy as an act of hospitality deeply resonates with me. The description of "hospitality as an expression of compassion" and how as therapists, we have the opportunity to show our clients this hospitality by providing safe, welcoming spaces, makes good sense to me. I appreciate some of the biblical references to hospitality, particularly the one where Abraham offered hospitality to the visiting strangers. To refer to the visitor as "stranger," I'm reminded of a conversation I had with Christine Pohl about hospitality. She said, "Perhaps we could say that [hospitality's] origin is in human vulnerability, sociality, and longings for community. As a stranger a person is often vulnerable, and when they're traveling, they're very dependent on the kindness of other strangers, other people whose community they're trying to enter. So I suspect that hospitality began as a form of mutual aid. . . . Everybody was, in a sense, vulnerable."[1] It's obvious to consider the visitor as a stranger, but unexpected to refer to the host as a stranger. And yet, in terms of that relationship, they, in fact, are strangers to one another. Typically, when we think about the visitor-host dynamic, we are aware of the imbalance of resources, placing the host in a position of advantage as she or he possesses a physical and social advantage over the visitor. The host is more likely to be in a posture of giving and the visitor in a posture of receiving and while that is certainly appropriate, if these roles are too rigidly held, there is a lost opportunity in mutual giving and receiving. But in this framework of hospitality presented by Dr. Pohl, both the visitor and the host are in positions of vulnerability *and* have mutual opportunity to be a blessing to the other.

1. Yoon Hammer, "Restoring Hospitality," 50.

Because I grew up in an immigrant family, the theme of hospitality has deep resonance for me. Although I was born in Canada and grew up in the United States, I had (and still have) countless experiences of being treated as a perpetual foreigner. My parents have now lived in North America for twice the number of years they lived in their homeland of Korea, but nevertheless we were and continue to be perceived and treated as foreigners. In so many ways the experience of hospitality was elusive, except in the Korean church. My family was deeply embedded in the Korean church which was, and still is, a thriving immigrant community and a place of hospitality—a gathering of visitors who became hosts to their fellow visitors. This is where my parents felt known and free in their own language and cultural practices. And this is where my family flourished. By no means was it perfect. It had its woes and challenges like any other immigrant church that eventually became multigenerational, but it was a safe, welcoming place for my family and me. This, I believe, is what the church is supposed to be for anyone, host or visitor. It is meant to be a place of safety and welcoming so that its congregants can be known and can flourish.

For my family, one of the most life-giving aspects of being part of the Korean community was the frequent gatherings that took place in homes and at church. My parents loved to host dinners and they did it often, making our home my first hospitality training ground. I enjoyed the warmth of our home filled with the aroma of good food and familiar voices, the entryway overflowing with shoes both inside and outside the door. I watched as the women entered our home, pulled back their sleeves, and started to cook together with my mom. And before they left, regardless of how late the hour, they packed up the food and cleaned the dishes. Our guests did not come only to be served, but also to serve, and by doing so, greater time and energy was spent on fellowshipping and less on hosting. As I got older I was expected to join in and help. I grew to appreciate learning to cook with my mother and her friends in the kitchen while listening to their stories and growing in my sense of connection and familiarity with my elders. I recognize that the culturally-informed gender dynamics that I'm describing here are not perfect and have the potential to be rigid and oppressive. But in the complexity of simultaneously holding both the beauty and the pain of some cultural traditions, I have gleaned a rich lesson about the gifts that can be found when there is a sense of mutuality and openness between the visitor and the host. What is recaptured and restored is the dignity and worth of the visitor who has something to offer. When we recognize this truth, we are more likely to cultivate an authentic compassion for the poor in spirit, the perpetual foreigner, the stranger, the other . . . the visitor because they are blessed . . . and are a blessing.

In a therapeutic relationship, there cannot be the same mutuality and vulnerability that is expected in nontherapeutic relationships. But I do think that what I'm talking about is applicable to therapists. Although our clients (the visitors) come to us (the hosts) for help, in essence, to receive a blessing, we too can be blessed by them. Even though we don't share the same degree of vulnerability with our clients that they share with us, the therapeutic use of self and compassion that moves us to self-disclosure and an exposure of our own humanity can enrich the blessing that goes both ways. Rachel Naomi Remen, a physician committed to restoring humanity in the practice of medicine stated it beautifully when she described the practitioner-patient encounter as follows: "We serve life not because we see it as broken but because we see it as holy. Of course, service itself is not a technique; it is a relationship—not a relationship between an expert and a problem but between two whole human beings who bring the full power of their combined humanity to a situation."[2] Therapeutic hospitality means we create a safe and welcoming space for our clients so that they might be blessed, while also remaining open and receptive to the ways they will bless us.

2. Horowitz, "Healing Patients and Physicians."

SABBATH REST

The final theme I would like to reflect on is Sabbath rest as a virtue and practice that helps restore communion with God and communion among us. Cameron has distinguished humility, hope, and compassion as virtues from Sabbath rest as a spiritual practice that supports them. While I would agree that among the four, Sabbath rest has the most obvious practical element, I would say that Sabbath rest is about presence as much as it is about practice and that the interplay between presence and practice becomes important. As pastor Mark Buchanan writes, "Sabbath is both time on a calendar and a disposition of the heart."[3] It is about both outward living and an inward orientation. On the one hand, Sabbath practice void of Sabbath presence results in hollow, meaningless actions that are driven by mere habit or legalism, being everything short of a blessing to the Sabbath observer. And on the other, Sabbath presence that isn't anchored in embodied practices can result in fleeting ideas that have difficulty taking hold of and bringing about meaningful change in our minds and our hearts.

Sabbath-keeping is a communal practice and, like any other practice, it gets more deeply embedded into individuals when it is observed, valued, and reinforced communally. Growing up in the Seventh-Day Adventist church and living in an SDA community, I was taught the importance of both Sabbath practice as well as Sabbath presence. In fact, in my own narrative, I would say that once I came to appreciate the beauty and richness of Sabbath rest and understand it to be a gift in both its practice and its presence, Sabbath turned out to be one of the most significant aspects of my family and community life that formed me in my identity as a Christian. I was taught at home and in school that Sabbath rest helps us remember that we are created beings, meant for rest, and that Sabbath was tied to gratitude for work as well as compassion for those who cannot rest. As a practice, the rhythm of family and community life was organized around the Sabbath. For example, on Fridays, school got out at noon so that we could go home and

3. Buchanan, *Rest of God*, 6.

prepare for the Sabbath. Stores closed an hour before sundown, and as the dusk hours rolled in every Friday it was as if the world started to quiet down and the frenetic energy that so often filled our home during the week began to dissipate. The practice and presence of Sabbath run deep. Down to the marrow of my bones I still feel the rhythm of Sabbath so that even though I no longer worship in the SDA church or live in an SDA community, my husband and I chose to continue Sabbath observance in our family and I still feel the shift on Friday afternoons during those dusk hours. There's a release and a welcoming that settles in, both in body and in spirit, in a way that doesn't happen any other day of the week.

And so, although I agree that Sabbath is "not simply an opportunity to get away from work," but rather to "cultivate a right relationship to our work," I will admit that I am profoundly appreciative of the opportunity to step away from the demands and pressures of work, for just one day. That's particularly true for those for whom work is less about job satisfaction or vocational fulfilment and more about mere survival, or those who work in conditions that challenge the assumptions of justice and dignity that others take for granted. If they are given the opportunity to have Sabbath rest, I agree that the rest ought to pose an opportunity for them to be restored in their relationship with God and to have a right relationship with their work. But I wonder what a right relationship with one's work is supposed to look like when the work and the workplace is oppressive. As Christians who believe that the Sabbath was created for us by a God who desires to restore us, how do we help the poor in spirit know the gift of Sabbath rest? How intentional are we in making sure that the lifestyles we maintain don't require a perpetuation of the kind of work that is oppressive for others? Sabbath rest brings us back to God but is also a means to bring us back to our awareness of others.

Cameron wrote that "Sabbath rest is an opportunity to remember who we are: the beloved children of a God who blesses the poor in spirit, who feeds those wandering in the desert." I agree that Sabbath rest, both as a practice and a presence, has the potential to restore our identity. Like the Jewish people for whom the Sabbath commandment was given as a gift to help restore them back to a right relationship with God after being in exile for so many generations, Sabbath rest helps us know ourselves rightly as people wholly dependent upon a God who continuously brings us back to him. As Christian therapists, we hold this truth as the wind that powers our work with clients. Some of us work in contexts that may not allow us to explicitly speak these words, but we believe that our clients are God's creation, wholly in need of the invitation to rest in his redemption. And so, we embody this first by practicing rest as we know ourselves rightly in the limitations of our own humanity. And we help our clients understand the limitations of their humanity, not as failures or shortcomings, but rather as the normal condition of being human. From the macro level of society to the cellular and molecular level of our physical being, rest is necessary for our health and for our relationships.

I'm grateful to have been part of this conversation. My hope is that the fruit born of these conversations will be that we might have compassion for ourselves and those who are meek; that we would be hospitable to the strangers in our midst, believing they will be a blessing to us as we are to them; and that we will rest in God, and in so doing, experience the restoration of our relationship with him and with one another.

POSTSCRIPT

Cameron Lee

I am deeply honored to have been asked to give the Integration Symposium lectures which form the core of this book. I am also honored that my colleagues have shared their wisdom in response. In a sense, the book embodies the way we stand shoulder to shoulder as co-laborers in a common task: the personal and professional formation of our students. But as slim as this volume is, it cannot do justice to what we are as a training program trying to accomplish. In this concluding postscript, therefore, I hope to accomplish two things. First, I want to bring the conversation full circle by "going meta" and responding briefly to my colleagues' responses. Second and finally, I want to share enough of the institutional backstory to create a historical context for how our program approaches integration, in the hope of helping our readers envision their own possibilities.

RESPONDING TO THE RESPONSES

Terry Hargrave

I appreciate the way Terry emphasizes the importance of the social and communal—not only for the sake of theory but for our pedagogy—in his response to my first lecture. As he has hinted in his essay, he already knows that I would agree.

When I have enough time to teach more fully from the diagram showing the focal/subsidiary and individual/communal dimensions of our theological formation, I usually describe something akin to what Terry calls a more "patterned" sequence of development. It has been said that being born into a family is like being thrust onto the stage of a play that is already in progress, and the same might be said of growing up in a church. In each case, there is already a shared history and narrative that (hopefully!) will make room for a child's individuality, but not by way of completely rewriting the script. We learn theology not only from the lessons that are explicitly taught, but from how the people around us live. That's not to say we're always aware of what we've internalized from these lessons. That may not happen until we find ourselves among people who have grown up with different traditions, and are forced to become focally aware of what was previously only subsidiary and to try to make sense of it all. People come to seminary and have what they have taken for granted held up unexpectedly to the light of day; over time, participation in this alternative community reshapes our subsidiary awareness.

As a result, you can't take the same language and ideas for granted any more. You can't listen to sermons and songs at your home church in the same way. For those being trained clinically, there's an added layer of complexity: you begin to see your family relationships differently. You can't play the same role in your family's dynamics without *knowing* that you're playing a role, which can be discomfiting.

For many people, therefore, and in many ways, the formative process of higher education means that you can't go home again.

So what do you do?

You smile and nod.

Not everyone, of course, experiences education in this way. Much depends, I imagine, on how curious we were as children, and how open our families and communities were to our questions. But the point here is twofold. First, even if the process of education opens one to disorienting new challenges, this struggle needs to be normalized as part of growth. Second, as Terry has emphasized, it's not enough to simply recognize that the struggle happens; it needs to become part of how we understand our pedagogical purpose. As those who would teach integration, we need to intentionally create a formational learning community in which people might struggle safely. I hope that my later comments in this postscript will make clear how my colleagues and I attempt to do this ourselves.

Pam King

I'm delighted with the preacher's sensibility and cadence in Pam's response; reading it is like listening to a rousing sermon on all that hope and humility should mean to us as believers. On the one hand, reading such laudatory comments from someone who was once my student is a little embarrassing. On the other hand, however, her comments help reinvigorate the hope and humility I need myself. Whatever I might think I'm doing when I stand up to teach, I may not be able to see what *God* is doing in that moment through my words, attitude, and actions—indeed, what God through his Spirit will continue to do. Thus, hearing her story in hindsight humbles me by giving me hopeful foresight. On any given day, in any given lecture, I might be tired, or distracted, or even a little discouraged. But it's not my job to move the universe. My responsibility is to show up with due diligence and faith, and to keep my primary and secondary callings in their proper order: *my* work is first *his* work.

Pam's description of hope is rich and multifaceted. Hope is weighty, like an anchor; it is sure, like a lifeline. It is not merely an intellectual abstraction or principle, but a living reality grounded in our covenant relationship with the God who delights in us as he delights in his Son. To see ourselves humbly is to embrace the truth of how God sees us *in Christ*, and embracing that truth gives us hope. Why? Because as both Michael Reeves and the apostle Paul have insisted, our participation in Christ is among other things participation in his resurrection (1 Cor 15:20–21).[1] It is the resurrection of Jesus that makes *Christian* hope specifically Christian.

Just as importantly, hope and humility must be embodied in our relationships to one another. As Pam has suggested, however life might rock our boats, we can trust that God has a firm hold on us. She speculates on how these virtues might be expressed in our secondary vocations of service. We can see and see clearly the God-given dignity and worth of others. We can invite them into God's story. We can encourage them to live in ways consistent with that story.

Drawing on Pam's emphasis on dependable relationship, I will say explicitly what I know she already believes: we must cultivate hope and humility not only in formal roles of service, but in the informal mutual service of the body of Christ, the church. I fear that in many of our congregations what we profess with our mouths to believe is betrayed by what we do in relationship to each other; we either do not know the larger story of God's restoration of *shalom* or else we give mere lip-service to it. We live in a world in which many stories compete for our narrative allegiance, and it is hard to hold the line on so grand a biblical narrative without a community of like-minded support. Whatever we as a seminary do, therefore, to shape the imaginations of our students while they are with us, it will need to be sustained by congregations and other Christian communities—communities of the resurrection—that dare to speak the language of humility and hope.

Miyoung Yoon Hammer

Miyoung's response rightly takes the perspective of the marginalized; in any and every age, these are indeed the ones whom Jesus would have called poor in spirit. It saddens me that as one who grew up in an immigrant family, she has so often felt marginalized herself. But it is also encouraging that Miyoung has known the

---

1. Reeves, *Rejoicing in Christ*.

rich and hospitable embrace of other believers, who have helped formed her imagination as a Christian and as a therapist.

I am fascinated by her idea of finding the courage to ask for healing in the midst of suffering. In the biblical stories she cites, "marginalized" would be a rough category at best. The woman with the hemorrhage, for example, would be a clearly marginal character: she was Jewish, female, and had a disorder that would make others ritually unclean. Jairus and the Roman centurion, however, had positions of influence in their respective social contexts. Esther's case is even more complicated: she was a member of a marginalized ethnic group who nevertheless found herself invested with power. But what unites these characters is their humility with respect to the only person who has the power to help their predicament, and their courage in making the approach.

The therapeutic implication is that those who seek a therapist's services—even if they seem ambivalent about being there!—are disempowered by their plight. As Miyoung notes, the compassionate therapist must blend empathy and action; again, as Kristen Neff has said, compassion entails that we see the suffering of others clearly, and want to do something about it.[2] But it matters what kind of action we take, and in what spirit. There is the professional who acts automatically from her position of privilege and attempts to "fix" her clients, and there is the one who realizes her privilege and seeks to empower them instead. The latter therapist knows how important it is for her clients to discover their voice, and strives to make sure that her compassionate action doesn't deprive them of it.

I wish that every Christian and every Christian therapist could have the same experience of hospitality that Miyoung has had. It's one thing to invite people to your home for a meal; it's another to have guests who behave in ways that bless the host even as they receive the host's hospitality! We are like the Emmaus disciples, inviting a new friend home for a bit of bread and good conversation, only to discover that it's Jesus sitting at table with us, when he suddenly takes over the role of host. A humble

2. Neff, *Self-Compassion*.

form of therapeutic compassion can recognize the power disparity between therapist and client while still hoping for a mutual blessing—because the therapist is attuned to what is holy in the other.

Finally, I appreciate Miyoung's emphasis on the interplay of presence and practice in sabbath rest; ultimately, you cannot have one without the other. She has something I do not: a personal history of the communal celebration of rest. She feels the sabbath rhythm in her bones; I know it in my mind and am still trying to get the message to the rest of my body. And she is right once again to bring up the matter of oppression, which, I take it, includes not only such matters as economic injustice but also the frequently inhuman expectations of economic success to which we are enslaved as a culture. How, she wonders, do we help the poor and oppressed experience sabbath rest, both practice and presence?

I wish there were a simple answer to such questions. But there is a clue, I think, in the notions of identity and embodiment. The sabbath commandment is indissolubly linked to our covenant identity; it is because we belong to *this* God and no other that we have rest as both commandment and gift. What we need, therefore, is to be embedded in covenant communities that continue to seek the face of the God of steadfast love even in the midst of oppression, including the oppression of work. As Miyoung suggests, it's not just about the practice of restful habits, put on in obedience to external rules; in the famous words of the seventeenth-century Carmelite monk Brother Lawrence, it's about practicing the presence of God. For that, we need communities of like-minded people who together can challenge the lies and half-truths we tell ourselves about work and worth, who can call us back to the God in whose presence alone we find our rest.

OUR PAST AND PRESENT

I have been training students at Fuller Seminary for over thirty years, teaching them family theory as they pursue psychotherapy licensure. Much has changed in that time, not only in the church at large and in psychology-related fields, but in the seminary (and indeed, in the nature of seminary education!) itself. When I first joined the faculty, I was part of the Department of Marriage and Family *Ministries*, under the institutional umbrella of the seminary's School of *Theology*. A year later, for a host of practical reasons, our program relocated to the School of *Psychology*, gradually growing into our new identity as the Department of Marital and Family *Therapy*. Formerly, we had understood ourselves as a ministry program, albeit with a license-eligible clinical emphasis. As such, we hadn't worried much about what our colleagues across the street in clinical psychology called "integration." But after the move, we were front and center a clinical program, wondering in what way our earlier ministry emphasis was still relevant.

Because I was the person with the most theological training in our department, it fell to me almost by default to figure out what integration would mean for us and our students. We experimented with a number of curricular arrangements. We tried having a single integration course at the beginning. Then we moved it to the end. Then we split it and had a course at the beginning *and* the end. We even tried—only once!—a marathon one-week format that simply left everyone completely spent. Each approach had its advantages and disadvantages.

But to me, what was lacking in every case was an overarching departmental vision. It wasn't enough to think in terms of filling a curricular niche, as if we were trying to meet an educational requirement for licensure. We needed a unifying sense of purpose. I imagined someone walking up to one of our alumni and asking this question: "So, I hear you did your clinical training at Fuller Seminary. What did they teach you? How was it any different from getting your degree from a state university?"

Would our students have a clear and ready answer? I was doubtful they would.

As we were wrestling with such questions, my teaching and preaching role at our church was expanding, which eventually led to my being licensed as a minister and appointed as a teaching pastor. For over twenty years now, I have been teaching a Bible class for an intergenerational fellowship in our congregation. My method is to teach entire books of the Bible, with verse by verse exposition—but not for the sake of increasing people's storehouse of biblical information. My goal has always been integrative and personal. Using my background in psychology (one member of the class refers to me jokingly as a "shrink"), I have sought to connect each lesson to people's lived experience in ways that would help them imagine themselves as part of the grand narrative of Scripture.

At last I began to realize that this was exactly what our clinical training program needed (better late than never). I don't mean that every course in the curriculum needed to become a Bible class. I mean that the curriculum as a whole needed a centering, biblical vision that would help students imagine how their clinical vocation might embody the biblical story.

The students who come to us have always represented a broad spectrum of personal and vocational clarity about pursuing clinical training. Many have known for a long time that they want to be therapists. Some have even heard an audible call or command from God and have come to fulfill what they already see as their destiny. Others, however, are not so sure. They have come to explore, to test the waters, to hang out the proverbial fleece.

Wherever students may be on that continuum of certainty, they often share one thing in common: an understanding of vocation as a black-and-white choice between career options, only one of which is the choice *God* wants them to make. This way of thinking, combined with an already well-ingrained performance mentality, tends to heighten their anxiety. Making the transition into graduate school is stressful enough. But it's even more stressful when less-than-optimal academic performance is interpreted as evidence that God disapproves of their career choice, or that they don't belong.

Thus the question: how might we teach integration in a way that most helpfully addresses such matters of vocational uncertainty and anxiety?

When I was studying and writing on Jesus' Beatitudes (Matt 5:3–12), I was struck with how just a handful of verses, understood in context, could encapsulate so much of Jesus' teaching about the kingdom of heaven. I began to teach from the Beatitudes in one of my seminary classes, developing the idea of "clinical virtues" that kingdom-minded Christians could cultivate and embody in their work with clients.

It seemed like a good start, but something was still missing.

That "something" was supplied by Terry Hargrave when he joined our faculty. I had been developing and teaching the concepts; Terry wanted to know what we could do better to bring them alive through a relational process of formation. From that conversation was born the formation process in which we engage now.

Here it is in brief. In their first fall quarter in the program, full-time students take a course from me in which they learn the overarching perspective of peacemaking and the clinical virtues introduced in this book. The goal is to capture the students' theological imaginations in such a way that they begin to see themselves as partners with God in the work of restoring peace to a broken world. This, I suggest, is their primary vocation: I encourage them to imagine themselves as agents of God's *shalom* in every situation and every relationship, whether in their family or church, the classroom or the clinic. Therapy then becomes one of many possible secondary vocations, arenas in which they may express their primary vocation as peacemakers.

I require students to interact weekly with course content by writing reflective essays in response to prearranged prompts. I have read hundreds of these essays over the years. It both delights and humbles me to witness how willing students are to write so deeply and honestly about themselves, and it encourages me in my own vocation to hear how challenging and yet liberating it is for them to begin understanding themselves as peacemakers.

In both the fall and winter quarters, students also participate in faculty-led small groups that meet weekly for the purpose of personal formation. In the fall, faculty members begin the group process by sharing the twists and turns of their own life stories. In subsequent weeks, the students follow suit. Many come to the program having been deeply hurt by their families and churches. The storytelling process begins to knit the students together into a community of humility, compassion, and hope in the face of pain. In the winter, formation groups continue to meet weekly, this time to discuss their written responses to prompts addressing each of the clinical virtues. Their responses become the springboard for further mutuality and conversation.

Finally, in the spring quarter of both their first and second years, the faculty and students meet off-campus for a one-day retreat. The day begins with student-led worship, followed by a time of private meditation and then group discussion centered on peacemaking and the clinical virtues. Lunch is generally a time of both fellowship and laughter, followed by more meditation and discussion. In recent years, students have also had the opportunity to observe a "fishbowl" with faculty at the center, engaged in a candid and personal discussion of one of the virtues. The day ends with a word of encouragement and prayer from the department chair. Students have often told us that at first, they felt too busy with their academic and clinical responsibilities to want to spend several hours on retreat; they have too many things to do! By the end of the day, however, they discovered that this was exactly what they needed—a time of rest and reflection to put all their busyness back into proper perspective.

These are our current practices. They are always under discussion and open to revision; by the time this book is in print, some of the practices may have changed. But what will not change is our shared vision, our commitment to helping our students learn what it means to be agents of God's peace in all they do, inside and outside the clinic. For to us, that is what integration means: integrity and wholeness, a coherent vision and story that holds together our primary and secondary vocations, all cultivated in community.

Pasadena, California
March, 2019

CONTRIBUTORS

Cameron Lee, PhD, CFLE, is Professor of Family Studies at Fuller Theological Seminary in Pasadena, California, where he has taught since 1986. He is a certified family life educator (CFLE) and licensed Family Wellness trainer, as well as a licensed minister and teaching pastor in the congregation where he is a member. His primary research interest is the lives of pastors and their families, and he has written and taught frequently on the subject. He also speaks and preaches regularly on topics related to relationships, marriages, and families, and has taught a weekly Bible class for over twenty years. In his writing ministry, he blogs three times weekly on Scripture and the Christian life at "Squinting Through Fog" (www.the-fog-blog.com) and is the sole or senior author of eight previous books, most recently, *What Love Does and Why It Matters: Romance, Relationships, and 1 Corinthians 13* (2017) and *Marriage PATH: Peacemaking at Home for Christian Couples* (2015). His professional articles have appeared in journals such as *Family Process, Family Relations, Journal of Psychology and Theology*, and *Journal for the Scientific Study of Religion.*

Terry D. Hargrave, PhD, is the Evelyn and Frank Freed Professor of Marriage and Family Therapy at Fuller Seminary, and is president of and in practice at Amarillo Family Institute, Inc. He is nationally recognized for his pioneering work with intergenerational families and is the co-founder of Restoration Therapy. He has authored over thirty professional articles and thirteen books, including *Advances and Techniques in Restoration Therapy* (co-authored with Nicole Zasowski and Miyoung Yoon Hammer), and *Families and Forgiveness: Healing Wounds in the Intergenerational Family* (2nd edition, co-authored with Nicole Zasowski). Dr. Hargrave has presented nationally and internationally on the concepts and processes of family and marriage restoration, intergenerational families, and aging. His work has been featured on *ABC News 20/20*, *Good Morning America*, and *CBS Early Morning*, as well as several national magazines and newspapers. He has been selected as a national conference plenary speaker and as a master's series therapist by the American Association for Marriage and Family Therapy.

Pamela Ebstyne King, PhD, is Peter L. Benson Associate Professor of Applied Developmental Science at Fuller Seminary. She works with the Thrive Center for Human Development in the School of Psychology. Her primary academic interests are applied research at the intersection of human thriving and spiritual development, and is a leader in the empirical study of religious and spiritual development within developmental psychology. Her research has been funded by Biologos Foundation, John Templeton Foundation, and Tyndale House. King is co-author of *The Reciprocating Self: Human Development in Theological Perspective*, co-editor of *The Handbook of Spiritual Development in Childhood and Adolescence*, and has served on the editorial boards of numerous academic journals. She is a member of the Society for Research on Adolescents, Society for Research on Child Development, and Division 36 of the American Psychological Association. She is ordained in the Presbyterian Church (USA), and speaks and consults regularly for churches and community organizations.

Miyoung Yoon Hammer, PhD, is Associate Professor of Marriage and Family Therapy at Fuller Seminary and chair of the Department of Marriage and Family Therapy. Prior to joining the faculty in 2009, she worked as a medical family therapist, providing therapy for patients and their families in hospital, outpatient, and private practice settings. She also served as an associate faculty member at the Chicago Center for Family Health. Currently, she teaches a course on medical family therapy, which focuses on working collaboratively with families and their healthcare practitioners. Her training and research interests also involve the personal and professional formation of the self of the therapist, helping students to better understand how their family and faith narratives inform their clinical work. Outside the classroom, she supervises students in the Restoration Therapy model. She is a member of the Collaborative Family Health Association, the California Association of Marriage and Family Therapists, and the American Family Therapy Academy. She is also a licensed marriage and family therapist in California and Illinois.

BIBLIOGRAPHY

Ahn, Hyun-nie, and Bruce E. Wampold. "Where Oh Where Are the Specific Ingredients? A Meta-Analysis of Component Studies in Counseling and Psychotherapy." *Journal of Counseling Psychology* 48 (2001) 251–57.

American Psychiatric Association. *Diagnostic and Statistical Manual of Mental Disorders.* 5th ed. Arlington: American Psychiatric, 2013.

Anderson, Harlene. *Conversation, Language, and Possibilities: A Postmodern Approach to Therapy.* New York: Basic, 1997.

Arras, John D. "Nice Story, But So What? Narrative and Justification in Ethics." In *Stories and Their Limits: Narrative Approaches to Bioethics,* edited by Hilde Lindemann Nelson, 65–88. New York: Routledge, 1997.

Ashton, Michael C., and Kibeom Lee. "Empirical, Theoretical, and Practical Advantages of the HEXACO Model of Personality Structure." *Personality and Social Psychology Review* 11 (2007) 150–66.

Ashton, Michael C., et al. "The HEXACO Honesty-Humility, Agreeableness, and Emotionality Factors: A Review of Research and Theory." *Personality and Social Psychology Review* 18 (2014) 139–52.

Baird, Katie, and Amanda C. Kracen. "Vicarious Traumatization and Secondary Traumatic Stress: A Research Synthesis." *Counselling Psychology Quarterly* 19 (2006) 181–88.

Baldwin, Scott A., et al. "Untangling the Alliance-Outcome Correlation: Exploring the Relative Importance of Therapist and Patient Variability in the Alliance." *Journal of Consulting and Clinical Psychology* 75 (2007) 842–52.

Balswick, Jack O., et al. *The Reciprocating Self: Human Development in Theological Perspective.* 2nd ed. Downers Grove: InterVarsity, 2016.

Barber, Jacques P., et al. "Alliance Predicts Patients' Outcome Beyond In-Treatment Change in Symptoms." *Journal of Consulting and Clinical Psychology* 68 (2000) 1027–32.

Bass, Dorothy. *Receiving the Day: Christian Practices for Opening the Gift of Time.* San Francisco: Jossey-Bass, 2000.

Beauchamp, Tom L., and James F. Childress. *Principles of Biomedical Ethics.* 7th ed. New York: Oxford University Press, 2013.

Beaumont, Elaine, et al. "Measuring Relationships Between Self-Compassion, Compassion Fatigue, Burnout and Well-Being in Student Counsellors and Student Cognitive Behavioural Psychotherapists: A Quantitative Survey." *Counselling and Psychotherapy Research* 16 (2016) 15–23.

Beilby, James K., and Paul R. Eddy, eds. *The Nature of the Atonement: Four Views.* Downers Grove: InterVarsity, 2006.

Bonhoeffer, Dietrich. *Letters and Papers from Prison.* London: SCM, 1971.

Bouma-Prediger, Steve. "The Task of Integration: A Modest Proposal." *Journal of Psychology and Theology* 18 (1990) 21–31.

Brody, Howard. *Stories of Sickness.* 2nd ed. Oxford: Oxford University Press, 2003.

Brueggemann, Walter. *Biblical Perspectives on Evangelism: Living in a Three-Storied Universe.* Nashville: Abingdon, 1993.

———. *Hope Within History.* Atlanta: John Knox, 1987.

———. *Peace.* St. Louis: Chalice, 2001.

———. *Sabbath as Resistance: Saying No to the Culture of Now.* Louisville: Westminster John Knox, 2014.

Bruner, Jerome S. *Acts of Meaning.* Cambridge: Harvard University Press, 1990.

Buchanan, Mark. *The Rest of God: Restoring Your Soul by Restoring Sabbath.* Nashville: Nelson, 2006.

Buechner, Frederick. *The Clown in the Belfry: Writings on Faith and Fiction.* San Francisco: Harper, 1992.

Charon, Rita. "Narrative and Medicine." *New England Journal of Medicine* 350 (2004) 862–64.

———. "Narrative Medicine: A Model for Empathy, Reflection, Profession, and Trust." *Journal of the American Medical Association* 286 (2001) 897–902.

Cheavens, Jennifer S., et al. "Hope Therapy in a Community Sample: A Pilot Investigation." *Social Indicators Research* 77 (2006) 61–78.

Connor, Dana R., and Jennifer L. Callahan. "Impact of Psychotherapist Expectations on Client Outcomes." *Psychotherapy* 52 (2015) 351–62.

Coppock, Timothy E., et al. "The Relationship Between Therapist and Client Hope with Therapy Outcomes." *Psychotherapy Research* 20 (2010) 619–26.

Costa, Paul T., Jr., and Robert R. McCrae. "The Five-Factor Model of Personality and its Relevance to Personality Disorders." *Journal of Personality Disorders* 6 (1992) 343–59.

Dawn, Marva. *Keeping the Sabbath Wholly: Ceasing, Resting, Embracing, Feasting.* Grand Rapids: Eerdmans, 1989.

DeSilva, David A. *Honor, Patronage, Kinship and Purity: Unlocking New Testament Culture.* Downers Grove: InterVarsity Academic, 2000.

Dew, Sarah E., and Leonard Bickman. "Client Expectancies about Therapy." *Mental Health Services Research* 7 (2005) 21–33.

Emmons, Robert A. *The Psychology of Ultimate Concerns: Motivation and Spirituality in Personality.* New York: Guilford, 1999.

Erikson, Erik H. *Identity, Youth, and Crisis.* New York: Norton, 1968.

Eysenck, Hans J. "The Effects of Psychotherapy: An Evaluation." *Journal of Consulting Psychology* 16 (1952) 319–24.

Figley, Charles R. "Compassion Fatigue: Psychotherapists' Chronic Lack of Self Care." *Journal of Clinical Psychology* 58 (2002) 1433–41.

Figley, Charles R., and Marne Ludick. "Secondary Traumatization and Compassion Fatigue." In *APA Handbook of Trauma Psychology: Foundations in Knowledge*, edited by Steven Gold, 573–93. Washington, DC: American Psychological Association, 2017.

Fowers, Blaine J. *Virtue and Psychology: Pursuing Excellence in Ordinary Practices.* Washington, DC: American Psychological Association, 2005.

Gawande, Atul. *Being Mortal: Medicine and What Matters in the End.* New York: Metropolitan, 2014.

Gergen, Kenneth. *Realities and Relationships: Soundings in Social Construction.* Cambridge: Harvard University Press, 1994.

Gold, Steven N., ed. *Handbook of Trauma Psychology, Volume 1.* Washington, DC: American Psychological Association, 2017.

Gottman, John M. *The Marriage Clinic: A Scientifically Based Marital Therapy.* New York: Norton, 1999.

Grade, Chaim. *My Mother's Sabbath Days.* Translated by Channa Kleinerman Goldstein and Inna Hecker Grade. New York: Knopf, 1986.

Gray, Alison J. "Attitude of the Public to Mental Health: A Church Congregation." *Mental Health, Religion & Culture* 4 (2001) 71–79.

Green, Joel B. "Kaleidoscopic View." In *The Nature of the Atonement: Four Views*, edited by James K. Beilby and Paul R. Eddy, 157–85. Downers Grove: InterVarsity, 2006.

Grenz, Stanley J. *Theology for the Community of God.* Nashville: Broadman & Holman, 1994.

Guinness, Os. *The Call: Finding and Fulfilling the Central Purpose of Your Life.* Nashville: W Publishing Group, 2003.

Habermas, Tilmann, and Cybèle de Silveira. "The Development of Global Coherence in Life Narratives Across Adolescence: Temporal, Causal, and Thematic Aspects." *Developmental Psychology* 44 (2008) 707–21.

Habermas, Tilmann, and Susan Bluck. "Getting a Life: The Emergence of the Life Story in Adolescence." *Psychological Bulletin* 126 (2000) 748–69.

Hargrave, Terry D. *The Essential Humility of Marriage: Honoring the Third Identity in Couples Therapy.* Phoenix: Zeig, Tucker, and Theisen, 2000.

Heschel, Abraham Joshua. *The Sabbath.* New York: Farrar, Straus & Giroux, 1951.

Hinshaw, Stephen P. *Another Kind of Madness: A Journey Through the Stigma and Hope of Mental Illness.* New York: St. Martin's, 2017.

Horowitz, Sala. "Healing Patients and Physicians: An Interview with Rachel Naomi Remen, MD, Pioneer in Mind-Body-Spirit Medicine." *Alternative and Complementary Therapies* 7 (2001) 149–53.

Irving, Lori M., et al. "The Relationship Between Hope and Outcomes at the Pretreatment, Beginning, and Later Phases of Psychotherapy." *Journal of Psychotherapy Integration* 14 (2004) 419–43.

Jecker, Nancy S., et al., eds. *Bioethics: An Introduction to the History, Methods, and Practice.* Sudbury: Jones and Bartlett, 2007.

Joinson, Carla. "Coping with Compassion Fatigue." *Nursing* 22 (1992) 116–21.

Jordan, Augustus E., and Naomi M. Meara. "Ethics and the Professional Practice of Psychologists: The Role of Virtues and Principles." *Professional Psychology: Research and Practice* 21 (1990) 107–14.

Killian, Kyle D. "Helping Till it Hurts? A Multimethod Study of Compassion Fatigue, Burnout, and Self-Care in Clinicians Working With Trauma Survivors." *Traumatology* 14 (2008) 32–44.

King, Pamela E. "The Reciprocating Self: Trinitarian and Christological Anthropologies of Being and Becoming." *Journal of Psychology and Christianity* 35 (2016) 215–32.

Knapp, Samuel, et al. "The Dark Side of Professional Ethics." *Professional Psychology: Research and Practice* 44 (2013) 371–77.

Kottler, Jeffrey. *Compassionate Therapy: Working with Difficult Clients.* San Francisco: Jossey Bass, 1992.

Kraybill, Donald. *The Upside-Down Kingdom.* Updated ed. Harrisonburg: Herald, 2011.

Labberton, Mark. *Called: The Crisis and Promise of Following Jesus Today.* Downers Grove: InterVarsity, 2014.

Lambert, Michael J. "Outcome in Psychotherapy: The Past and Important Advances." *Psychotherapy* 50 (2013) 42–51.

Larsen, Denise J., and Rachel Stege. "Hope-Focused Practices During Early Psychotherapy Sessions: Part I: Implicit Approaches." *Journal of Psychotherapy Integration* 20 (2010) 271–92.

———. "Hope-Focused Practices During Early Psychotherapy Sessions: Part II: Explicit Approaches." *Journal of Psychotherapy Integration* 20 (2010) 293–311.

Lee, Cameron. "Agency and Purpose in Narrative Therapy: Questioning the Postmodern Rejection of Metanarrative." *Journal of Psychology and Theology* 32 (2004) 221–31.

———. "Integration and the Christian Imagination." In *Integrating Faith and Psychology: Twelve Psychologists Tell Their Stories*, edited by Glendon L. Moriarty, 246–64. Downers Grove: InterVarsity, 2010.

———. *Marriage PATH: Peacemaking at Home for Christian Couples.* Pasadena: Fuller Institute for Relationship Education, 2015.

———. *Unexpected Blessing: Living the Countercultural Reality of the Beatitudes.* Downers Grove: InterVarsity, 2004.

Lopez, Shane. *Making Hope Happen: Create the Future You Want for Yourself and Others.* New York: Atria, 2013.

MacIntyre, Alasdair. *After Virtue.* 2nd ed. Notre Dame: University of Notre Dame, 1984.

Maiz, B. F. "This Love of Ours." Poem performed live at the Texas Association for Marriage and Family Therapists Annual Meeting, January 28, 1996.

Marchant, Jo. *Cure: A Journey into the Science of Mind Over Body.* New York: Crown, 2016.

Maslach, Christina. *Burnout: The Cost of Caring.* Reprint, Los Altos: Malor, 2015.

May, William F. "The Virtues in a Professional Setting." *Soundings* 67 (1984) 245–66.

McAdams, Dan P. *The Stories We Live By: Personal Myths and the Making of the Self.* New York: Guilford, 1993.

McCann, I. Lisa, and Laurie A. Pearlman. "Vicarious Traumatization: A Framework for Understanding the Psychological Effects of Working with Victims." *Journal of Traumatic Stress* 3 (1990) 131–49.

McCarthy, Joan. "Principlism or Narrative Ethics: Must We Choose Between Them?" *Medical Humanities* 29 (2003) 65–71.

Moriarty, Glendon L., ed. *Integrating Faith and Psychology.* Downers Grove: InterVarsity, 2010.

Mukherjee, Siddhartha. "Bodies at Rest and in Motion." *The New Yorker,* January 8, 2018.

Neff, Kristin. *Self-Compassion.* New York: Morrow, 2011.

Negash, Sesen, and Seda Sahin. "Compassion Fatigue in Marriage and Family Therapy: Implications for Therapists and Clients." *Journal of Marital and Family Therapy* 37 (2011) 9–10.

Nelson, Hilde Lindemann, ed. *Stories and Their Limits: Narrative Approaches to Bioethics.* New York: Routledge, 1997.

Neyrey, Jerome H. *Honor and Shame in the Gospel of Matthew.* Louisville: Westminster John Knox, 1998.

Norcross, John C. "Psychotherapist Self-Care: Practitioner-Tested, Research-Informed Strategies." *Professional Psychology: Research and Practice* 31 (2000) 710–13.

Nouwen, Henri. *The Wounded Healer.* Reprint, New York: Image, 1979.

Oden, Amy G., ed. *And You Welcomed Me: A Sourcebook on Hospitality in Early Christianity.* Nashville: Abingdon, 2001.

Okiishi, John C., et al. "An Analysis of Therapist Treatment Effects: Toward Providing Feedback to Individual Therapists on Their Clients' Psychotherapy Outcome." *Journal of Clinical Psychology* 62 (2006) 1157–72.

Paine, David R., et al. "Humility as a Psychotherapeutic Virtue: Spiritual, Philosophical, and Psychological Foundations." *Journal of Spirituality in Mental Health* 17 (2015) 3–25.

Pescosolido, Bernice A. "The Public Stigma of Mental Illness: What Do We Think; What Do We Know; What Can We Prove?" *Journal of Health and Social Behavior* 54 (2013) 1–21.

Peterson, Christopher, and Martin E. P. Seligman. *Character Strengths and Virtues: A Handbook and Classification*. Oxford: Oxford University Press, 2004.

Plantinga, Cornelius. *Not the Way It's Supposed to Be: A Breviary of Sin*. Grand Rapids: Eerdmans, 1995.

Polanyi, Michael. *Personal Knowledge: Towards a Post-Critical Philosophy*. Chicago: University of Chicago Press, 1962.

Polanyi, Michael, and Harry Prosch. *Meaning*. Chicago: University of Chicago Press, 1975.

Radden, Jennifer, and John Z. Sadler. "Character Virtues in Psychiatric Practice." *Harvard Review of Psychiatry* 16 (2008) 373–80.

Radeke, JoAnn T., and Michael J. Mahoney. "Comparing the Personal Lives of Psychotherapists and Research Psychologists." *Professional Psychology: Research and Practice* 31 (2000) 82–84.

Reeves, Michael. *Rejoicing in Christ*. Downers Grove: InterVarsity, 2015.

Rowden, Trampas J., et al. "Understanding Humility and Its Role in Relational Therapy." *Contemporary Family Therapy* 36 (2014) 380–91.

Sacks, Oliver. *The Man Who Mistook His Wife for a Hat*. New York: Touchstone, 1998.

Sandage, Steven J., et al. "Humility in Psychotherapy." In *Handbook of Humility: Theory, Research, and Applications*, edited by Everett L. Worthington et al., 301–15. New York: Routledge, 2017.

Seligman, Martin E. P. *Authentic Happiness*. New York: Free Press, 2002.

Skovholt, Thomas M., and Michelle Trotter-Mathison. *The Resilient Practitioner*. 3rd ed. New York: Routledge, 2016.

Smith, Mary Lee, et al. *The Benefits of Psychotherapy*. Baltimore: Johns Hopkins University Press, 1980.

Snyder, C. R. "Hope Theory: Rainbows in the Mind." *Psychological Inquiry* 13 (2002) 249–75.

Snyder, C. R., et al. "Hope Theory, Measurements, and Applications to School Psychology." *School Psychology Quarterly* 18 (2003) 122–39.

Snyder, C. R., et al. "The Will and the Ways: Development and Validation of an Individual-Differences Measure of Hope." *Journal of Personality and Social Psychology* 60 (1991) 570–85.

Stamm, Beth Hudnall. *The Concise ProQOL Manual*. 2nd ed. Pocatello: ProQOL.org, 2010.

Stamm, Beth Hudnall, ed. *Secondary Traumatic Stress*. 2nd ed. Baltimore: Sidran, 1999

Stanford, Matthew S., and Kandace R. McAlister. "Perceptions of Serious Mental Illness in the Local Church." *Journal of Religion, Disability & Health* 12 (2008) 144–53.

Strawn, Brad D., and Miyoung Yoon Hammer. "Spiritual Formation through Direction at Fuller Theological Seminary School of Psychology." *Journal of Psychology and Christianity* 32 (2013) 306–14.

Swift, Joshua K., and Annie O. Derthick. "Increasing Hope by Addressing Clients' Outcome Expectations." *Psychotherapy* 50 (2013) 284–87.

Tan, Siang-Yang. *Counseling and Psychotherapy: A Christian Perspective*. Grand Rapids: Baker, 2011.

Tangney, June Price. "Humility." In *Handbook of Positive Psychology*, edited by Shane J. Lopez and C. R. Snyder, 411–19. New York: Oxford University Press, 2002.

Teater, Martha, and John Ludgate. *Overcoming Compassion Fatigue: A Practical Resilience Workbook*. Eau Claire: PESI Publishing and Media, 2014. Kindle edition.

Turgoose, David, and Lucy Maddox. "Predictors of Compassion Fatigue in Mental Health Professionals: A Narrative Review." *Traumatology* 23 (2017) 172–85.

Walfish, Steven, et al. "An Investigation of Self-Assessment Bias in Mental Health Providers." *Psychological Reports* 110 (2012) 639–44.

Webb, Marcia. *Toward a Theology of Psychological Disorder*. Eugene: Cascade, 2017.

Williams, Rowan. *Being Disciples: Essentials of the Christian Life*. Grand Rapids: Eerdmans, 2016.

Winner, Lauren. *Mudhouse Sabbath: An Invitation to a Life of Spiritual Discipline*. Brewster: Paraclete, 2007.

Witherington, Ben, III. *Work: A Kingdom Perspective on Labor*. Grand Rapids: Eerdmans, 2011.

Worthington, Everett L., Jr., et al., eds. *Handbook of Humility: Theory, Research, and Applications*. New York: Routledge, 2017.

Yalom, Irvin D. *The Gift of Therapy: An Open Letter to a New Generation of Therapists and their Patients*. New York: HarperCollins, 2002.

Yoder, Perry B. *Shalom: The Bible's Word for Salvation, Justice, and Peace*. Reprint, Eugene: Wipf & Stock, 2017.

Yoon Hammer, Miyoung. "Restoring Hospitality: A Blessing for Visitor and Host: A Conversation with Christine Pohl." *Fuller Magazine*, 2016. https://fullerstudio.fuller.edu/wp-content/uploads/2017/01/FULL_Magazine-n06_Spring-16-lr2.pdf.